NEEDLERY

The Connoisseur's Album of Adventures in Needlepoint and Embroidery by Glenora Smith

Butterick Publishing

Editor
CAROL CASTELLANO

Photographer
EDWARD SCIBETTA

Illustrator
JANET LOMBARDO

Book Designer
SALLIE BALDWIN

All designs originated and executed by the author.

Library of Congress Catalog Card Number: 77-92604
International Standard Book Number: 0-88421-045-6
Copyright © 1978 by Butterick Publishing
161 Sixth Avenue, New York, New York 10013
A Division of American Can Company

PRINTED IN U.S.A.

Preface

When you sit in the silence
and listen to your soul,

    time is timeless

        place becomes space.

           And the music that you hear
           grows from within
           and echoes around
           the lives you hold most dear,
        for my children,
        for all those who shine.

Loving thanks to all those around me
who helped when I needed help,
who laughed when I needed laughter,
who cared when I could not,
who believed in a dream
and let me know that rainbows can be real!

Special thanks to all those who answered my endless questions
and contributed in their own way.
And to the "inner circle" at Butterick,
who have patience by the pound!

Contents

Introduction

Why *Needlery?* JOY! The simple pleasure of time with oneself, new avenues of self-discovery, challenge, adventure. Awaken your creative potential. Respond to demands on time and talent. Discover new and exhilerating directions.

Explore the quiet side of your soul,
make of yourself a beautiful space in which to live,
make of Life a beautiful place in which to travel;
discover there are no bounds, only more beginnings,
new facets, new horizons, new tomorrows
that you can savor today!

From traditional techniques a new art form, Needlery, was born. It encompasses an abundance of sensitivity and dimension: visual, emotional, intellectual. The aspects may differ, but the direction is the same . . . connoisseur. *Needlery* is a connoisseur's corner of design . . . color, creativity, imagination!

I realize that people have different levels of dexterity and enthusiasm. Some of us are quite zealous; others prefer not to jump into the deep end until they discover how well they can swim. I have categorized the twenty-six needlery pieces in the book according to the dexterity required to execute them. Level I introduces a few stitches with small, simple projects. Level II expands your stitchery knowledge with more complex projects. Level III explores the realm of needlery with projects requiring dedication and expertise. It is for those who realize the sky is the limit, for those who will not let the clouds interfere with a superb stitchery accomplishment!

PART ONE
Needlery Basics

Needlery is free-form stitchery which often combines needlepoint and embroidery. Needlery offers the freedom to explore a new realm of creativity. To enter this arena, it is important to master the basics of both needlepoint and embroidery.

The needlepoint information included in Needlery *is complete—from basics through finishing. The embroidery information is more specific, concentrating on techniques used in Part Two, Needlery Designs. Most embroidery in the projects is worked over needlepoint.*

Chapter One
Needlepoint Materials

Needlepoint, known in the past as canvas work, needle-tapestry, and cushion work, is the American term for a type of embroidery worked over vertical and horizontal evenly woven threads—traditionally canvas, linen, or wool. *Tapestry,* a European term, refers to earlier needlepoint works that were copies of fourteenth-century woven tapestries. These embroideries were most often worked in the Gobelin stitch, which was named for the famous tapestry weaver (see page 31). In the early nineteenth century, canvas embroidery became known as Berlin work. Today Europeans refer to it as canvas work.

Embroidery in America is best traced through the samplers which children made. They served the practical purpose of teaching children the alphabet and numbers and also pictured life in early colonial times. Often the subject of a sampler was a verse rather than a picture. Since there were no spelling books, and since samplers were often worked by children five or six years old, many of the results are quite amusing, although sampler making was considered a most serious task indeed. As the country became less harsh and living conditions improved, many crafters embroidered pictures of their homes on samplers and frequently embellished them with watercolors.

Today, needlepoint techniques know no bounds; needlepoint has become an exciting and unique art form. With full respect for tradition and the

proper execution of stitches, you can explore the endless possibilities of design, color, and texture that the variety of yarns and threads allow.

There are three categories of needlepoint, each worked on a different size canvas: *petit point,* small stitches usually worked on 16 mesh canvas (gauge: 16 canvas threads per inch) or smaller; *demipoint,* medium stitches usually worked on 10 to 15 mesh canvas (gauge: 10 to 15 canvas threads per inch); and *gros point,* large stitches usually worked on $3\frac{1}{2}$ to 7 mesh canvas (gauge: $3\frac{1}{2}$ to 7 canvas threads per inch).

Canvas

The many sizes and types of needlepoint canvas available allow for great variation and imagination in design and stitchery. You can work traditional designs on penelope canvas or appliqué unusual sections worked on gauze. Often the end use of the project determines the canvas you'll need.

Canvas is made up of long vertical threads, the *warp,* and short horizontal threads, the *weft* (often referred to as *woof*). Warp threads run the length of the canvas when the *selvages* (the finished edges of the canvas) are at the sides. Weft threads run across the canvas from selvage edge to selvage edge.

The *diagonal grain* runs from the upper left corner of the canvas to the lower right.

Working with the selvage at your left, so that the warp threads are in a vertical position, results in a more durable finished piece that will be less likely to pull out of shape when blocked.

The manufacturer adds starch called *sizing,* to the canvas. Just as canvas varies, so does the amount of sizing in it. Too much sizing creates an overly stiff canvas; too little sizing creates a limp and flimsy canvas. Buy wisely.

In general, canvas is 24 or 36 inches wide. The narrower width is usually a finer mesh, or size canvas. Canvas mesh ranges in size from a $3\frac{1}{2}$ (rug canvas) to 30 (fine gauze). The popular sizes for most projects are 12, 14, 16, and 18. To cut canvas evenly, follow the thread lines. It is important to cover the raw edges with masking tape, seam binding, or latex glue so the yarn won't catch on them.

MONO CANVAS

Mono is a plain-weave, single-thread canvas with evenly spaced warp and weft threads. It is the most versatile for design and handling and therefore the most popular. It has more give, so it is preferred for curves and shading. A good quality mono canvas has few knots, if any; it has a sheen indicative of the durable threads used and a uniform weave.

PENELOPE CANVAS

Penelope is a canvas with its double threads interlocked for firmness and strength. It is unique because the warp threads are woven closer together than the weft threads; the result is two different mesh sizes in one canvas. You can work over the single mesh for a petit-point result, or over the double mesh for a gros-point result (see page 10). When you are working the petit-point mesh, your design will be one-quarter the size of the gros-point design. You can use penelope for multiscale designs instead of appliquéing a smaller mesh canvas onto a larger mesh canvas. Traditionally, the design is worked over the single mesh threads, and the background over the double mesh threads; however, the opposite method is equally effective.

The most popular penelope is 10/20, but 12/24 and 7/14 are also available. Penelope canvas is necessary for stitches that require extra mesh for proper execution. There is also a penelope canvas specially woven for cross stitch. Be sure to buy the proper canvas for your project.

GAUZE

Gauze is a single-thread mono canvas with a very fine gauge, ranging from 30 to 40, that maintains body even though it is very fine. It is most often used for small sections of a piece, such as the face or hands of a figure, and then appliquéd to another piece of needlework done on a heavier mesh canvas.

PLASTIC CANVAS

A flexible but self-supportive canvas in 6 mesh only, plastic canvas is a limited medium; but its uniqueness lends itself to designs of an unusual nature. It is available in $10\frac{1}{2}$ by $13\frac{1}{2}$-inch sheets which are easily cut to smaller sizes.

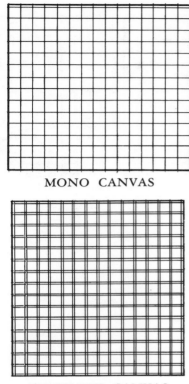

MONO CANVAS

PENELOPE CANVAS

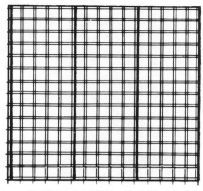

DISPOSABLE CANVAS

FABRICS

Needlepoint can be worked on even-weave fabrics. Linen is most often used, though cotton, wool, or even burlap have been used successfully. Burlap can add an interesting textural note when left exposed as an integral part of the design.

DISPOSABLE CANVAS

A double-weave canvas with blue vertical warp threads spaced ½ inch apart, disposable canvas is most often found in #14 mesh canvas. This canvas is solely for appliquéd sections. It doesn't work for an entire needlework piece because it is too flimsy.

Working Frame

Still a controversy on the needlework horizon, working frames are not a new device, although many people think they are. Many old museum pieces are still on their working frames. I favor frames for many reasons. It is easier to see the mesh so that you'll make fewer mistakes; both hands are left free. Speed and skill are increased when you can work with one hand on top of the canvas and one underneath and you do not have to struggle with holding the canvas. The result is more precise work: the finish is smoother, the tension of the stitches is uniform, the canvas does not pull out of shape. A **C** clamp can be used to secure your frame to a table while you're working.

A frame also makes it possible to work with more than one needle. You can pull your yarn to the front of the canvas and "park" it out of the way until you are ready to reuse that particular color. This technique is particularly useful for complex designs. I always use a frame, and I must admit that I think everyone else should too. When securing canvas to a frame, be sure the selvage is on the left side to insure the proper position of the canvas grain (warp threads in a vertical direction).

SCROLL FRAME

A scroll frame allows the needlework to roll up at either end while you work the center. It is best for a large canvas, such as rug, which would

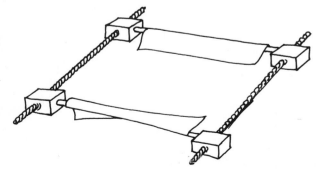

SCROLL FRAME

otherwise be too clumsy to handle. Hem 1 inch of the canvas across all raw edges; sew the hem to the webbing on the frame with heavy-duty thread and very large stitches. Scroll frames are available in small hand sizes, larger table sizes, and even larger floor models.

STRETCHER FRAME

A stretcher frame, traditionally used for stretching an artist's canvas, is a simple wooden frame with four precut pieces. It is available in assorted sizes. Purchase the size appropriate to your canvas and fit the four sections together at the mitered corners to form the frame. Be sure to choose a frame large enough to expose your entire design through the opening. Allow $1\frac{1}{2}$ to 2 inches of extra canvas beyond the design for proper blocking and finishing of your needlework. Attach the canvas directly to the frame (a staple gun works best), along the four sides.

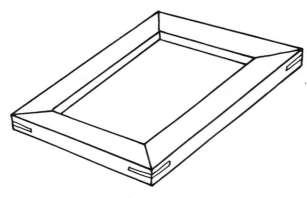

STRETCHER FRAME

Needles and Scissors

For your needlepoint, use a *tapestry needle,* a blunt-tipped needle which can pass between the canvas threads without splitting them. The larger the needle number, the smaller the size. The largest size is 14, the smallest size is 24. Choose the needle size according to the size of your canvas and yarn. With the proper size, the threads will not be distorted when the needle passes through the canvas.

Two kinds of scissors are needed: narrow, pointed embroidery shears that must be sharp and of good quality or they will "chew" your yarn, and a pair of larger, standard scissors for cutting the canvas. Canvas sizing tends to dull the blades, so don't use your embroidery shears to cut canvas.

Yarn

The choice of yarn is determined by the mesh of the canvas and the design and purpose of the finished product (which can range from a durable chair

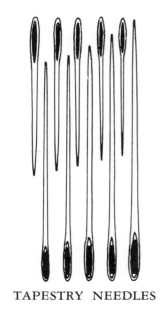

TAPESTRY NEEDLES

seat to a fragile wall hanging). If your canvas is a fine mesh, it needs a fine yarn; a larger mesh calls for a thicker yarn. In general, the more mesh threads per inch, the finer the yarn; the fewer mesh threads per inch, the thicker the yarn. If the yarn is too thick, it will distort the canvas threads. If the yarn is too thin, it will not cover the canvas satisfactorily. It is wise to work a test sample with the canvas and yarns you have chosen. Needlepoint yarn should have a long, smooth fiber with a loose twist. Yarns vary greatly, even within the same brand, because different color dyes take differently and thus the yarns work up differently on your canvas.

YARN VOCABULARY
Thread: A filament or fiber from which yarn is made.
Yarn: Any spun thread.
Strand: A single length of thread or yarn.
Ply: The number of twisted threads in one strand of yarn.
Skein: A small, coiled bundle of thread or yarn. Various yardages can equal one skein.
Working thread: That which you have threaded through your needle to work a specific stitch. It may be a single strand or several strands. It can be one type of yarn or different yarns combined to create the desired effect.
Tail: The thread end that is furthest from the eye of the needle.

TYPES OF YARN
persian wool
The most popular needlepoint yarn, Persian wool has three 2-ply threads per strand. The threads are easily separated; hence Persian wool is readily adaptable to different sizes of canvas and various designs. An excellent color range of over three hundred colors is available. The wool is sold by the strand, skein, hank, or ounce.

crewel wool
Crewel is a finer yarn than Persian, though the two are usually interchangeable. Since it is a 2-ply, one-thread strand, as many strands as the

design dictates can be used. Crewel wool is sold by the strand or by the ounce, but it is most commonly found in 20- to 25-yard skeins.

french wool

A very fine yarn, French wool is considered the best. It is not as springy or hairy as Persian, thus the strands settle in place very well. It is preferred by many for the soft patina it acquires with age. The color range is limited but exciting, for the color distinctions are sharp rather than dull, making it an excellent yarn for shading effects. It is quite versatile, and it is used for petit point and embroidery (see pages 10 and 41). A 2-ply, single-strand yarn, it is usually sold by weight.

tapestry wool

Many people refer to Persian yarn as tapestry yarn, but that is incorrect. Tapestry yarn is a heavier, rounded, 4-ply single-thread yarn. It is most often used for rugs or other surfaces that must be durable. Due to the physical characteristics of this yarn it cannot be separated to accomodate different size meshes. Hence it is used primarily on penelope canvas or other perfectly scaled canvas. It is available in a fairly wide color range, though there are few bright colors. It is sold by weight, by the yard, and by the skein.

rug wool

A very coarse, durable yarn, primarily used for rugs, rug wool is often referred to as rya yarn. However, rya yarn is only the best quality rug yarn, a very lustrous yarn quite distinguishable from other rug wool. Rug wool is a 4-ply single-thread yarn which does not separate well. The color range is quite limited; consider this when you plan your design. Rug wool is sold by the pound (approximately 250 yards) or by the skein.

knitting wool

Knitting wool is not recommended for needlepoint. The best yarn for needlepoint has long fibers, giving a smooth effect, and knitting yarn has short fibers, making it less durable, wiry, and springy. An unsatisfactory hairy effect results, since the fibers often break down as the stitches rub

against the canvas threads. Since there are so many beautiful, fine quality, varied wools on the market today, it seems foolish to use a less than satisfactory material. Remember, it is your time, talent, and treasure at stake!

silk twist

A tightly twisted 2-ply yarn, silk twist is expensive, but a small amount is most effective. The most popular twists are imported from England and France and sold on cards in 8-yard skeins. Hand-dyed silk twist is by far the most beautiful, for the natural striations and shadings in the yarn are still apparent after dying, giving your work more depth and character. It is often dyed with subtle ombre shadings which are quite a dramatic addition to a needlework piece. Hand-dyed silk twist is sold by the ounce or in 10-yard skeins. Manufacturer-dyed twist comes in a wide color range; the hand-dyed color range is virtually limitless.

silk floss

Silk floss is a very fine 2-ply yarn of six threads per strand. A word of warning: it's like working with spider webs! However, if you handle it carefully the final effect is well worth it. Beeswax is most helpful in controlling its flyaway characteristic (see page 19); but be careful not to coat your yarn too heavily, or it will lose the full effect that silk floss can offer. Silk floss is available in the same brilliant color range as the imported silk twist, and the use of the same color in the two different yarn types is quite exciting. Silk floss is sold in 4-yard skeins.

french silk

Like French wool, French silk is considered to be of the highest quality. It is a 2-ply yarn, with eight threads per strand. The price often prohibits its use for an entire project, but do consider it for special effects. It has a very special feel. Its characteristic sheen and depth of color are incomparable. It lies beautifully on the canvas, compliments your needlery technique, and shows the stitches to their best advantage. It is superb! French silk is sold by the skein.

cotton floss

Cotton embroidery floss is a 2-ply yarn, six threads per strand. The fiber is mercerized cotton. It is of a finer scale and smoother texture than wool. It is easily separated; in fact, you should separate the threads of each strand prior to use, to insure a uniform finish of flat threads. You can easily add more threads to make the proper thickness for different sizes of canvas, and they blend well. Mouline has a sheen and durability not found in other cotton yarns. Hence, it is often substituted for silk. The color range is immense, exciting, and inspiring! Cotton floss is sold in 8.7-yard skeins for a very nominal fee.

cotton tapestry yarn

Cotton tapestry yarn is not mercerized, and it lacks the sheen of cotton floss. It is a heavier, 5-ply single-thread yarn. It cannot be separated and the color range is very small. It is recommended for use only on #14 canvas. Cotton tapestry yarn is sold in 10-meter (approximately 11-yard) skeins.

perle cotton

A French mercerized cotton yarn available in three weights (#1, #3, #5), Perle is a 2-ply single-thread yarn which does not separate. However, the variety of yarn weights makes this yarn quite versatile anyway. The color range is coordinated on a limited basis with that of the cotton floss. The color numbers are the same; thus a textural contrast is easily achieved. Perle cotton is sold in 53-yard balls or 27.3-yard skeins.

european linen

European linen is a very fine 2-ply single-strand yarn. The quality is excellent. The colors are soft and muted. One associates them with European canvas work. When worked, it has a marvelous old world quality, and it blends beautifully with antique furnishings. It is sold in 15-yard skeins.

domestic linen

Made from a cruder flax than European linen, domestic linen has more pronounced slubs and looks less refined. It is available in two weights: 10/5, the heavy weight yarn with a 5-ply single strand, and 20/2, the light weight yarn with a 2-ply single strand. Its very crude quality can add an interesting primitive feeling to some designs. The color range is limited, and so is its use. It is sold in 15-yard skeins.

YARNS FOR SPECIAL EFFECTS
marlitt

Imported from Germany, Marlitt is a 2-ply yarn with 4 threads per strand. The finish is like glass, and just as dramatic. It is very springy to work and frays easily, but a small dab of white glue on the end will control it. The color range is absolutely vibrant! It is sold in 10-meter (approximately 11-yard) skeins.

metallics

Yes, they are actually made of metal: copper, gold, silver, and antique silver. This is not a yarn for the novice; it requires a great deal of dexterity and patience in handling. A couching technique (see page 45) is often necessary; however, the finer threads can be used directly on the canvas.

Metallic yarns are imported primarily in a 3-ply single-strand yarn, in a weight comparable to heavy buttonhole twist. Metallics are also available in the synthetic lurex, but these do not age and tarnish like the true metallics do. All metallics except Japanese gold tarnish. Japanese gold is actual gold leaf on paper coiled around a silk core.

mohair

True mohair yarn is made from the long, silky hair of the angora goat, but a similar yarn is now being made from a mixture of wool and rayon. Mohair is a 2- or 3-ply single-strand yarn with brushed fibers that create a hairy effect. It is available in numerous colors and quantities from knitting shops or speciality-yarn suppliers.

synthetics

A word of caution: some synthetics get fuzzy, others pull apart; some

are superb, others are only good in small areas for special effects. Try to find out about the limitations of the particular yarn you are considering. In general, they lack the characteristics of the yarns they simulate. Because the characteristics of synthetics vary so greatly, it is wise to use only those I have listed under the specific projects.

THE RECOMMENDED APPROACH

• When you experiment with yarns, work with fewer threads rather than more. You can always add another thread and work over the area again. Too much yarn forces the mesh together and makes spaces uneven. Too little yarn does not cover the canvas properly and leaves canvas threads exposed. Through experimentation with fibers, canvas, and stitches, you can discover the best yarn for the best results in a particular design.

• Yarn colors work up darker than they appear. Therefore contrasts may not show up as you had hoped. A test sample is always advisable.

• Yarns vary a great deal in color and texture, even those from the same manufacturer. Thickness as well as dye lot will affect your needlework. It is advisable to use the same yarn throughout your needlework project.

• Beeswax, the natural wax from which bees make their honeycomb, is used to tame the finer flyaway threads (such as silk floss) and to prevent snagging or tangling and make it less wispy to work. Beeswax is sold in small pieces or in convenient cases with notches through which to run your thread. Be sure not to coat your thread too heavily or you will lose the effect of the fine yarns.

BEESWAX

ESTIMATING YARN

The amount of yarn required for a design depends on the size of the canvas, the mesh of the canvas, and the stitches to be used. The same stitch has a different effect when worked on mesh of different sizes or with different

yarns. To estimate the amount of yarn required, work a 1-inch square in the stitch and yarn you intend to use. Measure the amount of yarn needed to complete the square inch. Count the number of square inches to be covered and multiply it by the amount of yarn used in your sample. Divide this figure by the yardage of each skein. Be sure to be generous, especially on a background color that you may not be able to match later.

The following yarn charts can be used as a guide in estimating the amount of yarn required for a project. However, since there are so many variables, it is wise to make the 1-inch square sample. The charts refer to coverage per square inch for basketweave-stitched areas.

Paternayan yarn: 40 34″ strands equal 1 hank (approximately 1 ounce)
       10 34″ strands equal 1 skein (approximately $\frac{1}{4}$ ounce)
Based on the use of one 3-ply 34″ strand.

ply	3	2	2	2	1
mesh	#10	#12	#14	#16	#18
inches	4.5	6	4.5	3.25	6.5

(prepared by Betty Fuld of Black Sheep, Rye, New York)

Medici yarn: 400 54″ strands equal 1 hank (approximately $1\frac{3}{4}$ ounces)
    100 54″ strands equal 1 skein (approximately $\frac{7}{8}$ ounce)
Based on the use of one 54″ strand.

ply	6	5	4	4	3
mesh	#10	#12	#14	#16	#18
inches	1.18	1	.95	.9	.88

(prepared by Naomi Appleman of Crafts Gallery, Ltd., South Nyack, New York)

Where to Begin? Often one hears the retort "at the beginning," but that only leads to the question, "where is the beginning?" I feel that the design determines the direction one should take. Design dictates color and texture as well as shape. Once these factors are well defined, a few systematic guidelines will insure ease in the execution of that design.

BINDING RAW CANVAS EDGES

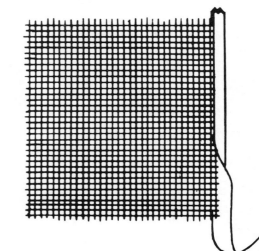

Counting

Count the threads of the canvas, not the holes, as a guideline. If you try to count the holes, it becomes most confusing. Each hole accomodates two or more stitches, but each thread is covered by only one stitch. All counting references in this book are based on *counting threads.*

Estimating Materials

Estimate the mesh and amount of canvas your design requires allowing $1\frac{1}{2}$ to 2 inches for a border. Cut the canvas to the proper size for the working frame. Prepare the raw edges by covering them with tape, seam binding, or latex glue. This keeps the canvas threads from fraying and the yarn from snagging on the edges. To cut the canvas evenly, follow the thread lines (see Canvas, page 10).

Estimate the amount of yarn needed for the design and background according to yarn weight and canvas mesh. Make a 1-inch square test sample (see Estimating Yarns, page 19, and Yarn, page 13).

Transferring the Design

CARBON

Dressmaker's carbon is a special carbon paper made for use on fabric. It is available in a packet containing various sizes and colors wherever sewing notions are sold. Do not use typewriter carbon to transfer a design. It will smudge as you work and ruin your fabric.

PRICK AND POUNCE

First transfer the design to heavy tracing paper. Place the drawing on a piece of felt or similar soft fabric. Then make a pricker from a needle jammed through a cork or large eraser. Prick tiny holes through the design drawing. If the pattern is detailed, make the holes close together.

Place the background fabric on a hard surface; place pricked transfer on top of it and secure in position. With pounce powder (powdered charcoal) and a blackboard eraser rub the powder gently through the holes. Use a small amount of powder at a time to get a clear impression. Remove the tracing paper, and gently blow off the excess powder.

With a small watercolor brush and gouache paint (available at art supply stores) or an indelible pen which has been tested for its water solubility, connect the powder dots, filling in the lines between the dots. Shake off any remaining powder, but do not attempt to rub it off for it will smudge.

TRACING

The design can be traced directly onto translucent embroidery background fabric. Tape the design to a window; tape the background fabric over it and make sure they do not shift. Trace the design with a fine line, using a light color indelible pen or a hard lead pencil.

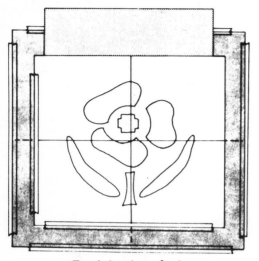

*Positioning design
and carbon for tracing*

TEMPLATES

Most often used in patchwork, templates are readily adapted to embroidery, if your design is a repetitive one. Draw the design on cardboard, cut out the shape along the outline, and trace the shape onto your background fabric.

DRAWING

To draw the lines of your design, use an indelible pen with ink that is *not* water soluble (so that it won't stain your needlework when it is dampened and blocked). A light color is best because it won't show through the yarn and cast a shadow on the finished needlework. A hard lead pencil can also be used, but not a soft lead pencil, since the lead rubs off on the yarn and soils it. On finer mesh canvas, sewing thread can be used to baste in an outline. You can stitch right over it and you don't have to remove it. Again, use a light color. For large canvas areas, use acrylic paints.

border

Leave a border of 1½ to 2 inches beyond the design outline for possible changes and ease in blocking and finishing. Mark the top of your canvas before you begin to stitch. This prevents you from working the stitches in the wrong direction, a common error in multistitch designs.

Attach the canvas to an appropriate working frame (see Working Frame, page 12) with selvages on the sides.

Working Your Needlepoint Project

THREADING THE NEEDLE

Wrap the yarn once around the needle and pull it taut; remove the needle while pinching the yarn tightly between your thumb and forefinger. Place the eye of the needle over the yarn, instead of forcing the yarn through the needle.

STARTING

Make a knot in the tail of your working thread. Place the knot on top of

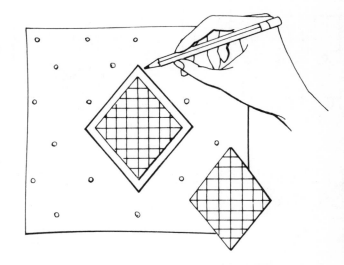

TRACING WITH TEMPLATES

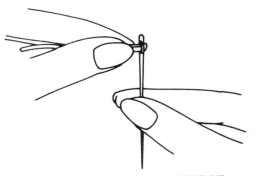

THREADING THE NEEDLE

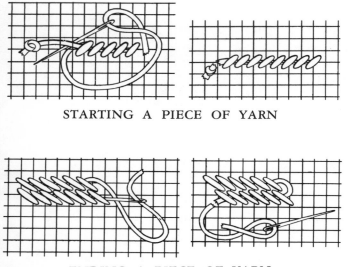

STARTING A PIECE OF YARN

ENDING A PIECE OF YARN

the canvas; start your needlework 2 inches away, and work toward the knot, thereby overcasting the tail thread as you work. Cut off the knot and any excess yarn.

STOPPING

Run the yarn under the stitches on the back of the canvas; take an additional back stitch to secure it, and cut off the excess yarn. Never end a dark color under a lighter color; it will cast a shadow on the front.

DIRECTION

Work from the center of the canvas to the outer edge, to make sure the canvas does not become misshapen and the threads are not hidden. If you plan to work a large area a little at a time, leave the worked portions with an uneven edge so "seams" will not appear and the stitches will blend. For geometric designs, work the outline of the predominant design first, then the rest of the design.

RIPPING OUT

Use a pair of narrow, pointed embroidery scissors with short blades. Snip in the direction in which you stitched to expose the canvas more easily. Cut threads on the back of the work where stitches are usually longer. The back will also expose the tails of other areas already completed; since the hidden tail is the anchor for the working thread, you must be careful not to snip the tail of another yarn while ripping out an area. Pull out threads by slipping the eye of the needle under the stitches on the right side; be careful not to snag adjacent stitches. It is imperative that you remove all the fuzz from the yarn you rip out, or it will discolor the yarn you newly work. Dampen your fingers slightly and rub hard over the exposed canvas; the leftover fuzz should roll into a ball for easy removal.

Technical Vocabulary

COMPENSATING STITCHES

To conform to a design it is sometimes necessary to make only a portion of a stitch. There may be areas where there are not enough canvas threads for you to execute the entire stitch.

RHYTHM

Rhythm refers to bargello—the up and down geometric pattern produced by the upright stitches (see page 28). The first row of the pattern defines the rhythm; each row builds upon the previous row.

SCOTCH METHOD

The Scotch method economizes on certain yarns, such as metallic or silk, because of bulk, difficulty in handling, or cost. Instead of taking a full stitch on the back of the canvas, take a short stitch into the next hole on the back of the work, thereby saving the length of thread required to cover the canvas back. This method is not recommended except where expense demands it; you might sacrifice the quality and durability of the finished design.

TRAMÉ

Tramé is a foundation for other stitches. It is an understitching done in an irregular pattern (to avoid ridges). On penelope canvas, lay tramé over the closely woven horizontal threads; it is often part of the canvas design when you purchase a ready made canvas. On a mono canvas, work tramé over vertical threads in a horizontal direction. Skip 2 horizontal threads between tramé rows.

Tramé can be laid as a padding in any area where a more full-bodied stitch is desired. Some stitches work easily over tramé. The straight Gobelin is one. When traméd it becomes the renaissance stitch.

Always lay all the tramé, and then overlay the stitch. It is wise to split the tramé stitches as you work for a smoother underlay and a more uniform effect when the overlay stitch is executed.

Tramé is a useful color guide, too, particularly in designing on a large canvas; tramé the areas in your chosen colors to make final decisions on color balance, shape, and overall design. Tramé can be used to create astounding results: in certain ecclesiastical and museum pieces colorful silk tramé threads overlap with gold and silver threads.

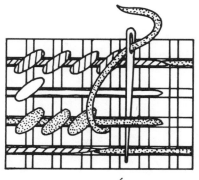

BARGELLO RHYTHM

TRAMÉ

TWEEDING

Two different color yarns can be used to obtain a third color, and two different types of yarn can be used to obtain a third texture. The tweeding method can be effective if the end result you desire is a mottled effect. See, for example, the look of the cobblestones in *Xmas* (Color Plate X) or the lion's fur in *King* (Color Plate K). This technique was also used for the subtle color difference in the sand for *Nautilus* (Color Plate N) and for the diffused sunset in *Eagle* (Color Plate E). Tweeding is not recommended for the subtle shading that leaves and flowers require; the result can seem gimmicky.

THE RECOMMENDED APPROACH

• Wool lengths (working threads) should not be cut too long, for the wool wears out as it is pulled through the abrasive canvas threads. The first stitches will be full-bodied, but the last stitches will be thin and scrawny. Use a 12-inch length for petit point, an 18-inch length for demipoint, and a 24-inch length for gros point (see page 10).

• Keep the tension even to insure a smooth, uniform finish. Stitches that are too tight will pull the canvas out of shape and expose its threads. Stitches that are too loose will shift position and look sloppy.

• Keep the canvas back neat. The neatness of the back contributes toward the finished look of the front: bits of wool and fuzz and threads from the back can catch in front stitches, and working threads can tangle.

• Occasionally, let your working thread dangle loose from your work to allow it to untwist. This is particularly important with diagonal stitches. Keep all stitches flat, for once twisted, they are impossible to untwist and they mar the textural finish of your needlework.

Chapter Three
Executing Needlepoint

Traditionally, the knowledge of needlepoint was a guarded family secret, recorded only on personal samplers handed down through the generations. Therefore, there is very little written description of the execution of the ancient stitches. There are hundreds of stitches; yet one cannot identify the few from which all others are derived. The basic stitches fall into two categories: long or short and tied or untied.

It is claimed by many that the tent stitch is the oldest; but then again, it may simply have been one of the most popular. The Egyptians used this slanted, durable stitch for sewing tents together. The cross-stitch is also an ancient stitch, as are the chain and satin stitches. Museum pieces tell us that the basic stitches are the same today as they were in antiquity. But needlery has grown to a new peak, and I feel it is a new beginning. Although many stitches mark important historic facts and many are centuries old, why not, occasionally, create your own?

Sampler

A sampler is a project in and of itself—a stitchery dictionary worked in a variety of stitches and patterns. Centuries ago samplers were the only record of stitches available to the needleworker. The courts of Italy, France, and

England maintained several samplers which served as teaching aids for generations of needleworkers. Many of these museum pieces are still an inspiration to us today.

Now it's your turn. Experiment! Make your sampler an exciting piece of needlework. One way to include all the aspects of design—color, texture, shape—is to choose a geometric pattern from a simple graphic painting or fabric and work this predefined design in your own colors and in various stitches. The more adventuresome needleworkers can just let the stitches flow and dictate their own design. Whatever your choice, it is wise to code the sampler as a future reference for the various stitches used.

Needlepoint Stitches

Needlepoint stitches are intended to resemble tapestry, and needlepoint works are often referred to, incorrectly, as tapestries. The design of a tapestry is created with the warp and weft threads by the weaver. In needlepoint, the tent and Gobelin stitches were used to imitate the tapestry designs. There are several versions of the versatile and popular tent and Gobelin stitches.

BARGELLO STITCH

Bargello is a classic ancient stitch which has come to be synonymous with flame and Florentine stitches. It is a long straight Gobelin (see page 31) or upright stitch (never crossed) that is worked over a specific number of threads in a designated rhythm (repeated up and down geometric pattern). The stitches are worked on the horizontal or vertical grain of the canvas.

A full-bodied yarn will cover the canvas better than a tightly twisted yarn since the bargello stitches are long and narrow.

Traditionally, bargello rhythms or patterns are worked in a few colors with several shades of each color echoing the outline. However, you can create fascinating interplays using different colors in the rhythm.

The first row of your pattern defines the rhythm that will be followed.

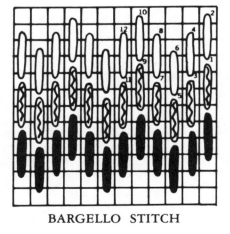

BARGELLO STITCH

Each row builds upon the previous row, but changes take place as the geometric progression takes place. Part of the fun of bargello stitchery is that it allows an element of spontaneity. The varieties and patterns are endless. Take the basic principles and play with them. The most basic rhythm is that of 4/2: each stitch covers four canvas threads, with a step of two canvas threads for each successive stitch above or below.

BASKETWEAVE STITCH

For backgrounds or other large areas, the basketweave stitch is recommended. It is sometimes referred to as the diagonal tent stitch. The name basketweave comes from the woven pattern produced on the canvas back. It is worked on the diagonal grain of the canvas instead of the horizontal. The rows dovetail together for a smooth finish; one settles well into the other without ridges. The advantages of the basketweave stitch are that it does not pull the canvas out of shape, it can be worked without turning the canvas, and it is one of the most durable stitches. Its limitation lies in the fact that it is not very maneuverable around curves and in small design areas.

BRICK STITCH

Each alternating straight brick stitch overlaps the previous stitch halfway, making each row dovetail into the previous row. The finished effect is that of laid bricks, hence the name. It is most durable when worked over two threads. It can be worked over four canvas threads as a background stitch. The size of your brick stitch should be in keeping with the scale of your design.

CONTINENTAL STITCH

The continental stitch is a tent stitch worked back and forth horizontally across the canvas, starting at the upper right. Working thus, from right to left, you must turn the canvas each time you start a new row. This stitch has certain disadvantages. It pulls the canvas badly out of shape, and no matter how well it is worked, ridges and imperfections occur which do not always disappear after blocking. The continental stitch is best used in moderation—on small areas or where its maneuverability is needed.

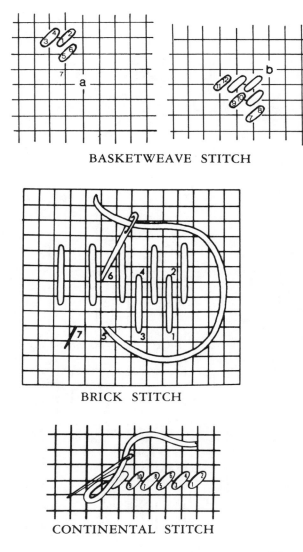

BASKETWEAVE STITCH

BRICK STITCH

CONTINENTAL STITCH

29

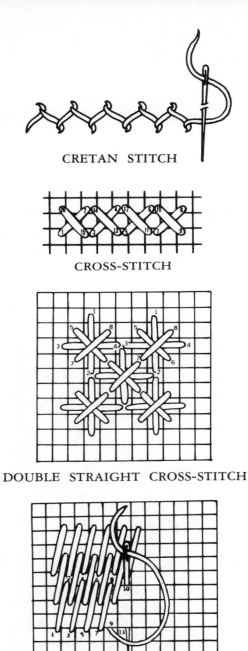

CRETAN STITCH

CROSS-STITCH

DOUBLE STRAIGHT CROSS-STITCH

ENCROACHING GOBELIN

CRETAN STITCH

Very different effects are attainable by varying the angle of the Cretan stitches and the spaces between them. When working on canvas keep the stitches close together for better coverage.

CROSS-STITCH

Cross-stitch can refer to a category of stitches in which the yarn is crossed in execution. However, the classic cross-stitch from which many others are derived, is a short two-step diagonal stitch. The first step is the tent stitch; the second step is the same stitch repeated with the slant in the opposite direction, over the same warp and weft threads. An **X**, or cross, is formed at the intersection of the canvas threads.

When you work the cross-stitch be sure all the **X**s cross in the same direction. When working on penelope canvas, you can work an entire row in step 1, then work the same row with step 2. On mono canvas, it is essential to work each stitch in two steps as you go, to hold the stitches properly in place.

Many museum pieces are worked solely in cross-stitch.

DOUBLE STRAIGHT CROSS-STITCH

This stitch consists of two crosses worked one on top of the other at ninety degree angles. The arms of the lower cross can be equal to or longer than the arms of the upper cross.

ENCROACHING GOBELIN STITCH

The encroaching Gobelin is also known as interlocking Gobelin. Each vertical row encroaches on one canvas thread of the previous row, parallel to the previous stitch, to give an interlocked appearance. It is usually worked over three, four, or five threads. This stitch tends to pull the canvas out of shape, but it is an excellent stitch for shading since it blends beautifully. Each row overlaps the previous row and produces a subtle color change rather than the sharpness of one distinct shade followed by another.

ENCROACHING OBLIQUE STITCH

The oblique is simply a version of the encroaching Gobelin stitch worked in a horizontal direction. It is an excellent background stitch. It is worked over four vertical threads and down one horizontal thread to form a long diagonal stitch. This stitch does not require as much yarn as the encroaching Gobelin.

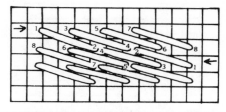

ENCROACHING OBLIQUE STITCH

GOBELIN STITCH

The Gobelin stitch, also called Droit, upright, straight, or satin stitch, is an upright stitch which imitates the ridges of woven tapestry. It is worked right to left, and you must rotate your canvas for each row. The tension should be kept uniform but not tight or the canvas threads will be exposed. You can work backstitch between the rows to cover exposed canvas threads and/or add color and texture. The number of canvas threads you cover depends on your design and the effect you desire.

GOBELIN
STITCH

HALF CROSS-STITCH

A tent stitch worked on penelope canvas, the half cross-stitch is extremely limited. It requires the double threads of penelope canvas to keep it from sliding out of position and becoming distorted; it does not provide a durable backing; and it pulls the canvas out of shape. Also, the half cross-stitch is worked from left to right, so you must turn the canvas for each new row, as with the continental.

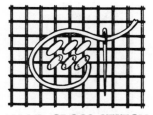

HALF CROSS-STITCH

HUNGARIAN STITCH

The Hungarian stitch is a combination of long and short stitches. Each series of three stitches forms a small diamond. The rows are alternating lines of equal-length short stitches over two threads and long stitches over four threads.

KNOTTED STITCH

The knotted stitch is often referred to as the French stitch (not to be confused with the French knot). It is a two-step stitch: the first step is a long diagonal stitch, the second step is a short tie-down diagonal stitch. It is also an encroaching stitch, for each row overlaps the previous row by one canvas thread. This stitch produces a finish that has a heavier texture than the encroaching Gobelin or encroaching oblique, and it has a relatively snag-proof surface.

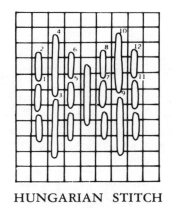

HUNGARIAN STITCH

31

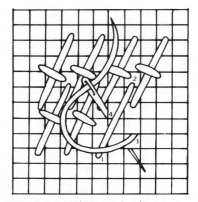

KNOTTED (FRENCH) STITCH

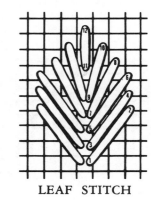

LEAF STITCH

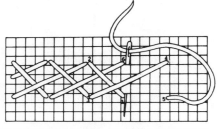

LONG-ARMED CROSS-STITCH

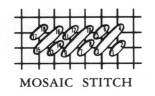

MOSAIC STITCH

LEAF STITCH

Eleven long stitches make up the leaf-shaped stitch. The tip of each stitch interlocks with the sides of the next two stitches. An upright stitch can be added at the center for a stem. You can make the leaf stitch larger or smaller by varying the number of canvas threads covered and the number of veins in each leaf. This stitch is particularly effective when worked in various shades of one color to simulate natural leaves.

LONG-ARMED CROSS-STITCH

While the long-armed cross is known as the Greek stitch, it is the stitch used exclusively in Tvistsöm, Swedish canvas embroidery. The finished stitch appears to be braided. It has become popular as a border stitch or a rug stitch. Although the back is scanty, the stitch is quite snag proof.

MOSAIC STITCH

The mosaic stitch is three short diagonal stitches per pattern unit. The second, a longer stitch, is between the shorter first and third stitches, forming a square. The stitches form diagonal rows across the needlework piece. The stitch is started at the upper left corner and worked toward the lower right corner. The tension should be kept uniform but not too tight, for like other diagonal stitches, the mosaic tends to pull the canvas out of shape. It is quite effective when worked in two colors or shades for a checkerboard effect.

ROCOCO STITCH

Rococo is a tie-down stitch that gives a fancy, lacy result that is great for Victoriana. It is a multistitch pattern unit consisting of four or six upright stitches which share the same hole at top and bottom; each stitch is tied down at the center with a single horizontal stitch over one canvas thread. It is worked in diagonal rows; each row dovetails with the previous row. It is very important, for the full impact of this stitch, to force the mesh open wide enough to accommodate the yarn and still give the appearance of open work. The yarn should be pulled taut as you work and the tension should be kept uniform or the holes will appear to be different sizes.

TENT STITCH

The basic stitch in needlepoint is the versatile and popular tent stitch. It is a short stitch which covers one intersection of warp and weft threads with a single diagonal stitch angled to the right. The three basic varieties of a tent stitch are the continental, the basketweave, and the half cross-stitch.

TURKEY WORK

Turkey work is also known as the Ghiordes knot, which was worked by hand into ancient woven rugs. Its tied down loops can be cut, left uncut, or sculptured for unique effects (such as in the ancient Chinese rugs). The size of the loops determines the depth of the pile. The stitch is started in the lower left corner and worked in horizontal rows back and forth. It is of limited use, but quite dramatic for animal fur, grass, flowers, or as a border fringe.

WHEAT STITCH

The wheat stitch resembles sheaves of wheat. It is made by working four or six upright stitches over four or six vertical threads followed by a single horizontal stitch over two or three threads across the center. A contrasting color is often worked in the spaces between the sheaves in an upright Gobelin or upright cross-stitch.

BACKSTITCH

Not technically a needlepoint stitch, the backstitch is often used to highlight or outline portions of a design. It is also used to fill in canvas between stitches such as the upright Gobelin or leaf stitch, which tend to expose a portion of canvas threads.

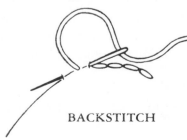

BACKSTITCH

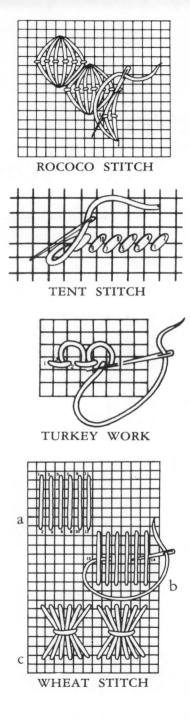

ROCOCO STITCH

TENT STITCH

TURKEY WORK

WHEAT STITCH

33

Chapter Four
Finishing Needlepoint

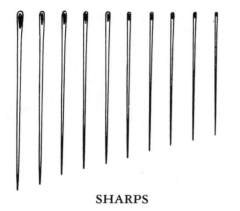

SHARPS

Choose the techniques which best suit the purpose of your needlework piece and the condition of your canvas. Work precisely, or the work will have to be repeated, ripped, or redone—a nightmare!

Finishing Materials

SEWING NEEDLES

Known as sharps, sewing needles have a smaller eye than tapestry needles; they are long and narrower and have a very sharp point. A sewing needle is needed to penetrate the thickness of the canvas and yarn in finishing.

CURVED NEEDLE

Often referred to as upholsters' needles, curved needles come in many sizes. Choose one appropriate to your project. The needle is curved for easier handling of awkward angles. The point is extremely sharp; be careful!

BEADING NEEDLE

Needles used for threading beads and sewing them onto the needlework are very thin and extra long. They have an extremely narrow eye and a sharp point which aids in picking up the beads.

BLOCKING BOARD

For a surface on which to block your needlework, choose insulation board, soft pine, or bulletin board or drawing board material—something not too hard for pins to penetrate. Mark the board with waterproof ink into 1-inch squares, or cover it with 1-inch-squared gingham. Align the gingham perfectly with the edges of the board. It is wise to spray the surface with an acrylic spray to insure a nonabsorbent working area. If you use gingham, underline it with foil.

PINS

Use stainless steel **T** pins from a knitting shop, wig pins from your local drug store, or aluminum pushpins (drawing pins) from an art supply store. Make sure your pins or tacks are rust proof.

CANVAS PLIERS

Most art supply stores carry pliers. Size #1 suits the purpose of blocking. You may not always need them, but they are superb for getting a grip on canvas edges when you are straightening your canvas.

MEASURES: T SQUARE, RULERS, TRIANGLE

Do not rely on your cloth tape measure. Most likely, it is not accurate, as it can stretch with use. A **T** square and a rigid ruler are far more reliable. A plastic see-through triangle is an asset in squaring corners. All can be purchased at art supply stores.

RABBIT-SKIN GLUE

Most often used for sizing artists' canvases, in needlework, rabbit-skin glue is used to retain the needlework's shape after blocking. It is not a must, but you will be wise to use it if your canvas will receive a great deal of wear, for example, if it will be used as a chair seat. The glue is available at art stores.

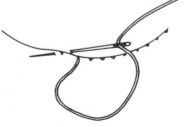

BINDING STITCH

SLIP STITCH

INTERLINING

Interlining adds more durability and body to your finished piece, which can become limp with wear. Choose the interlining according to what the end use of your project will be.

Finishing Techniques

BINDING STITCH

The binding stitch is often known as round braid or border stitch. It is worked at the edge of the canvas over two threads to give a smooth finish on a hemmed piece of needlework, such as a wall hanging. The yarn wraps around the canvas to bind it as you stitch from hole to hole. Use a double strand of yarn to insure the proper coverage of canvas threads and a full-bodied edge.

SLIP STITCHING

A series of small sewing stitches is done by hand from the right side of the needlework. These are used for appliqué, pillow closures, trim, and general overall finishing touches. It is wise to choose the same color thread as the last row of needlework so that the stitches will show less. A curved needle (page 34) is helpful in reaching difficult areas.

CURVED CANVAS EDGES

To finish curved canvas edges, topstitch (see page 37) at the edge of the needlework as close to the stitches as possible without stitching through the needlework. Run another row of machine stitches $\frac{1}{4}$ inch from the first row. Follow with a row of long (gathering) stitches which will gather the canvas easily. Leave the thread ends long so you can draw up the gathering and turn the canvas edges toward the back. This technique keeps large lumpy pleats from forming on the back of the canvas. Such pleats can cause ripples in the front of the needlework.

MITERING

The corners of the canvas are mitered for a smoother edge and less bulk. First, make a 45-degree fold of the corner point toward the center; then fold the top and bottom edges toward the center, creating a diagonal seam that is flush on all sides.

STAY STITCHING

A row of machine stitching or hand backstitching, stay stitching is done to secure the raw edges of the finished work so that it will not ravel. This is a must for all articles of clothing and other items that will be handled a great deal (such as pillows). Do not sew each edge continuously around the square, because the presser foot will force the canvas out of alignment. Sew two edges starting from the same corner; the other two edges, from the diagonally opposite corner.

TOPSTITCHING

Topstitching is machine stitching done on the right side of the needlework along the edges of a specified area, such as an appliqué patch or some special portion of the design.

THE RECOMMENDED APPROACH

• The finer the canvas mesh, the easier it is to handle during blocking; it is closer to fabric weight and will give less resistance.

• Hold your finished needlework piece up to a strong light and attend to any missed stitches you might discover.

• Always clip the selvage of the canvas so it will give during the pull-and-pin pull-and-pin process of blocking (page 38).

• When dampening, do not submerge the canvas as this will remove the sizing that helps hold the stitches in place and keeps the canvas in shape after blocking.

• Block all pieces keeping the grain of the canvas squared, no matter what the shape of the finished piece. If you have an odd-shaped piece,

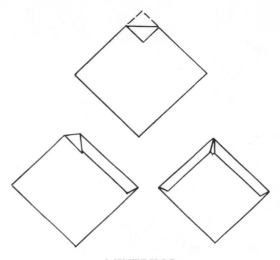

MITERING

block it before you cut it out. If it is blocked unevenly, it will never stay in shape.

• Do not remove pins until the piece is thoroughly dry or it will spring back and dry misshapen. The piece will feel dry to the touch long before the unexposed areas are dry. Let it dry in a light, well-ventilated area for from twenty-four to thirty-six hours. Do not try to hasten the process by placing the needlework in the sun or near a heat source; it might mildew, or worse yet, the heat might "cook" the wool and ruin it!

• If a canvas is badly distorted, you may have to repeat the blocking process several times.

Blocking

DAMPENING
Dampen the back of the canvas with a clean sponge and water. This loosens the sizing in the canvas, allows you to reset the canvas threads, and locks the threads into the new position when the canvas dries. Lay the dampened canvas on the blocking board—face down for most pieces (to make the stitches more uniform) but face up for pieces with heavy textural stitches.

If you have a particularly stubborn piece, let steam do the work; it will soften the sizing so you can pull the piece into shape as you are blocking. But do not use steam heat when blocking silk because it will cause dry rot; simply dampen instead.

PINNING
Pull the canvas diagonally, starting with the two corners that are the most askew. Use rustproof pins or tacks at the corners. Then divide and subdivide the spaces between the pins. Pull and pin, pull and pin, until the pins are about $\frac{1}{2}$ inch apart. Adjust as you pin until all edges are in the proper position. Use a **T** square or triangle to insure perfect 90-degree angles on pieces that will be framed. Don't get carried away and jam the pins in too deeply or you will go crazy trying to get them out.

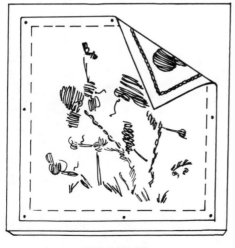

PINNING

Warning! If the pins are not close enough together, the edges will develop a scallop. Like a ripple in a pond, the scallop will affect the threads throughout the needlework piece and will force it out of line.

Let the canvas dry in position for at least two days, three days for a large piece.

STEAMING

Blocking evens up the stitches and tends to make them uniform; however, it also flattens them and can make your needlework lack depth. Steaming fluffs the surface and gives your piece a finished look.

Place the needlework face up. Hold a steam iron above the surface of the work. Do not touch the surface with the iron or it will flatten the stitches and defeat your purpose.

SIZING

The main purpose of sizing is to make sure the canvas maintains its shape after blocking. However, if you used a working frame, there is little chance the tension or stitches will cause a misshapen canvas. If your project is going to receive a great deal of wear (a chair seat, for example), sizing is recommended.

For smaller, decorative projects spray starch or a spray adhesive applied to the canvas back may be sufficient. If starch or adhesive is not enough, use rabbit-skin glue (see page 35). This glue makes the canvas quite stiff and is not recommended for clothing. Follow the preparation instructions on the tin carefully. Brush a thin coat over the entire back of the needlework, after the canvas is completely dry and before removing it from the blocking board.

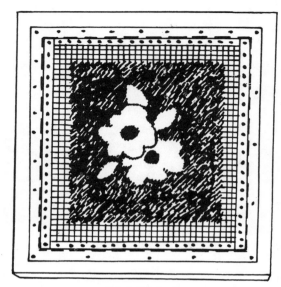

BLOCKING

Framing

MATS

Mats are traditionally worked in needlepoint in colors and textures that contrast with the picture background. The mat can be worked in the same stitches turned in a different direction (Gobelin and brick stitches work well). If you choose this technique, keep the proportion of threads the same; for example, if the background is worked over four threads, work the mat over four threads. You might like a soft fabric as a mat. Traditional picture mats can be used as well. The possibilities are there for you to play with and explore.

GLASS

It is not advisable to use glass to cover your needlework because wool must breathe and glass prevents this. Wool is affected by heat and dampness, and it will rot and fade beneath glass. If you must use glass (on a tray, for example), leave a space between it and the needlework, and wherever possible, leave the back open. Let the purpose of the project dictate the decision. The use of glare-proof glass is a matter of taste; some prefer it, some do not. Unfortunately, such glass is not available in a very thick size, so use caution when covering trays, desks, or tables.

FRAMES

Use a secure frame mounting since some pieces (such as those that are diagonally stitched) have a tendency to shift after blocking. A needlework piece must be perfectly blocked if it is going to be framed.

PROFESSIONALS

Don't hesitate to use the services of a good professional, especially if your project is a piece of furniture or a special picture. There are professional upholsterers and framers who will do an excellent job. Professionals need not know anything about needlepoint, but they must know their own craft well.

Of course, if you enjoy a challenge (hopefully you are a perfectionist), tackle the project yourself. There are courses (often at the "Y") in which you can learn framing and other finishing techniques. But if you are not confident of your ability in this area, it is best to go to a professional.

Chapter Five
Embroidery Basics

Embroidery stitches are worked over a fabric background to create raised and ornamental designs. (Needlepoint stitches create the design and background themselves.) Since you do not have to conform to a canvas grid, your embroidery stitches can be quite flowing and artistic in the interpretation of a design.

Unfortunately, the fragile nature of ancient embroideries has left us with a great deal of confusion as to the origins of stitches, yarns, and fabrics used. The few pieces which did survive (some have been found in the Egyptian tombs) have been difficult to document, forcing historians to use secondary sources, such as paintings, descriptive diaries, or household inventories.

Ecclesiastical embroidery, primarily done in convents and monasteries, predominated for centuries; embroidered heraldic and military designs followed. Mary, Queen of Scots, was a prominent figure in the evolution of embroidery. Her very lovely embroidery designs inspired crafters and made embroidery widely popular. During the reign of Elizabeth I, steel needles came into being, replacing bone needles. Steel needles allowed more precise and refined stitching and were easy to use. These characteristics further enhanced the popularity of embroidery. Soon pattern books such as *A*

Schole-Howse for the Needle, published in 1624, were available; and proper finishing schools included a course in needlework.

Traditional crewel work was done with 2-ply wool yarn on linen in pastel floral and pastoral designs. Yarn was not available for purchase to American embroiderers (as it was to Europeans), so they had to spin and dye their own yarns. The New World needleworker discovered new dimensions, new colors, new textures, and a whole new approach to needlework. This New World approach has led to today's more open, freer interpretations of traditional techniques. Though it is freer, and different, this New World approach is in no way less refined.

Embroidery Materials

BACKGROUND FABRIC

Let the purpose of the project dictate the background fabric. For a fragile wall hanging, use fragile materials; for a footstool or seat cover, use durable materials. Embroidery was traditionally stitched on linen, but there are really no limitations, save your imagination. Wool, silk, burlap, and denim are welcome. The general rules are that the fabric should be firmly woven and the threads should separate as the needle passes through them. When you work embroidery over needlework, the needlework becomes the background fabric.

YARN

Your fabric choice dictates whether the yarn you choose will be heavy or light in weight, bright or dark in color, hard or soft in texture, shiny or dull in finish. Keep in mind that these factors influence your design—which is the master of ceremonies and the end purpose of your work. Yarn choice is far more flexible in embroidery than in needlepoint since you are not limited by mesh size. You can use yarn of single, double, or triple strands, as you desire. You can also couch other yarns atop your background (see page 45). There are so many possibilities!

NEEDLE

If your needle is too small, your thread fibers will break down or become fuzzy and separate. If your needle is too large, your stitches will be irregular and hard to control. Choose a needle according to the yarn thickness and the weave of your fabric. The needle should have a sharp point, not a blunt point like a tapestry needle. Embroidery needles are sized from 2, largest, to 24, smallest.

FRAMES

A ring frame or embroidery hoop is still the most popular frame, undoubtedly due to its easy assembly and portability. As embroidery knowledge soars, however, more people are becoming aware of the variety of frames to choose from—including standing floor frames, quilting frames, square frames.

If you work embroidery over needlepoint, keep the work mounted in the needlepoint frame until all the stitchery is completed. Do not try to force needlepoint into an embroidery hoop when you wish to embellish it with additional stitchery; it will crush the background stitches and force the warp and weft threads out of position. If you embroider directly onto needlepoint canvas, do not use a hoop.

EMBROIDERY NEEDLES

Working Your Embroidery Project

ESTIMATING MATERIALS

In estimating the amount of materials needed, remember that the background fabric piece must be large enough to accomodate the design and the frame. The yarn type and needle size used are determined by the dimensions and purpose of the design. Refer to Estimating Yarns, page 19, to estimate the amount of yarn needed.

PREPARING THE FABRIC

Dressmaker's carbon is the simplest and most versatile means of transferring the design onto your background fabric. Work on a hard surface,

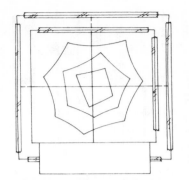

POSITIONING DESIGN
AND CARBON FOR TRACING

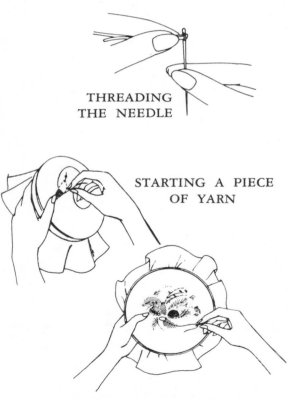

THREADING
THE NEEDLE

STARTING A PIECE
OF YARN

ENDING A PIECE OF YARN

tracing the embroidery design through the carbon paper onto the fabric. Or you can use the prick and pounce method (see Transferring the Design, page 22).

Set the background fabric into the embroidery frame of your choice. The dimensions and purpose of the design as well as personal preference determine what kind of frame is appropriate. When you work embroidery over needlepoint, leave the needlepoint piece in the working frame. Do not transfer it to an embroidery hoop; this will crush the canvas and distort the stitches.

THREADING THE NEEDLE

Wrap the thread around the eye of the needle and pull it taut. Remove the needle, pinch the thread between your thumb and forefinger, then slide the needle eye over the thread. Be sure the needle goes *between* the threads of your fabric instead of *through* them. Splitting the threads makes them weak.

STARTING

Begin your work with a small backstitch on the wrong side, or slip your thread through the back of previous stitches. Be sure to clip the tails to keep the back of your needlework neat! Don't use knots; they result in a lumpy surface when your piece is finished and blocked.

STOPPING

To finish a working thread, end the last stitch on the wrong side of the needlework and weave the needle back and forth through previous embroidery. Secure it with a small backstitch. Clip off excess yarn close to the fabric.

FINISHING

For methods of blocking and finishing your embroidered needlepoint, see page 34.

Technical Vocabulary

COUCHING

Couching is a technique in which the thread is laid on the surface of the background material and held in place by small tie-down stitches. Plain couching is done with a small, simple, straight stitch holding the surface yarn in place. Fancy couching is done with any of the fancy embroidery stitches or a combination of stitches.

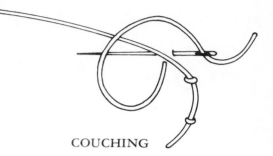

COUCHING

STABBING

Using a frame enables you to develop the two-handed up and down rhythm of the stabbing technique. One hand works above the needlework, one hand works below (since both hands are freed by the frame). This produces work that is more refined and accurate. With patience and practice, you will achieve speed and dexterity by working in this manner—and produce exquisite results as well!

THE RECOMMENDED APPROACH

- The best way to explore the world of embroidery is to work a sampler. You will not only learn all the basics, but you will have a future reference for color, texture, and stitchery (see Sampler, page 27).

- Simplify—in every facet of your embroidery—or the very essence of the design, color, and texture will be lost. Too much of anything, even your favorite dessert, is not pleasant. An embroidery design can easily be overwhelmed by too zealous a worker. Let the subtle interplay of color and texture stand on its own.

- A well-worked embroidery piece has a clean, precise quality about it. To attain this, keep your tension even, your needle vertical (not on an angle), your threads flat (not twisted), and your points well defined (by extending the stitch slightly beyond the outline).

- Work the dominant sections of your design first. If design sections overlap, work the underportion first.

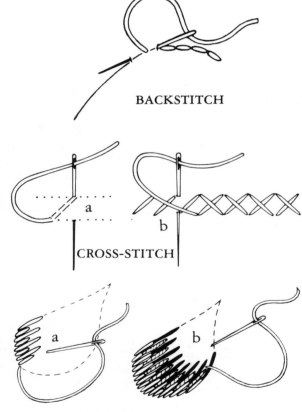

BACKSTITCH

CROSS-STITCH

LONG AND SHORT STITCHES

Embroidery Stitches

Embroidery stitches are beautiful, adaptable, versatile. They can be stitched anywhere on your fabric without restriction—unlike needlepoint stitches, which require the mesh and weave of canvas. You can work some embroidery—satin stitches, cross-stitches, French knots—directly on needlepoint canvas. Others—lazy daisy, feather, running stitches—require a fabric or needlepoint background.

Explore and experiment. In working any given stitch, you will discover that simple changes in the color and texture of the yarn and in scale will give that stitch a myriad of design possibilities. There are hundreds of stitches, and the variations are endless.

Flat stitches are the simplest stitches to execute. The term *flat* means that the stitches always lie on the surface of the background fabric.

BACKSTITCH

Backstitches form a line of even stitches with no spaces between them. Backstitches can be threaded with additional yarn (see Threaded Running Stitch, page 47).

CROSS-STITCH

The embroidery cross-stitch is executed in the same manner as the needlepoint cross-stitch (page 30). It is a short two-step diagonal stitch. The first step is a small stitch at a 45-degree angle. The second step is the same stitch repeated with the slant in the opposite direction. Be sure that all the **X**s cross in the same direction.

LONG AND SHORT STITCHES

Long and short stitches are most often used for shading. They are worked in alternate long and short lengths.

RUNNING STITCH

Running stitches form a line of even stitches in which the length of the stitches equals the amount of space between them. This line of stitches can be straight or curved.

SATIN STITCH

Satin stitches are a series of stitches which lie side by side to form a smooth well defined area. The stitches can be flat, couched (see page 45), or padded (several layers of satin stitches worked in different directions).

THREADED RUNNING STITCH

Working with a blunt needle, and often with a yarn of a contrasting color, weave an additional thread through a row of running stitches. Different patterns evolve depending on the tension of the stitches and the angle of weaving. You can also weave in opposite directions to create ovals.

Loop stitches are executed by looping the thread under the point of the needle before completing each stitch.

BUTTONHOLE STITCH

Probably the most familiar loop stitch, the buttonhole is often referred to as the blanket stitch (being used most often to bind blanket edges).

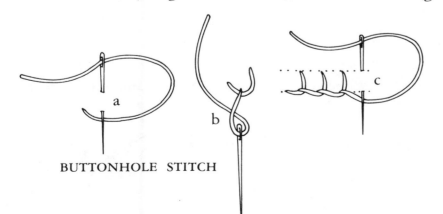

BUTTONHOLE STITCH

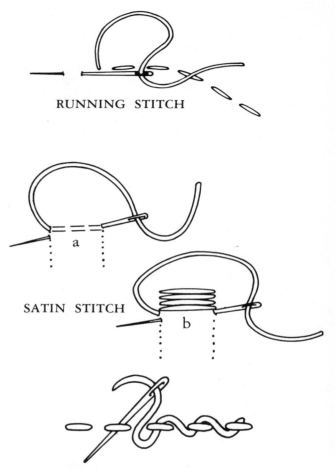

RUNNING STITCH

SATIN STITCH

THREADED RUNNING STITCH

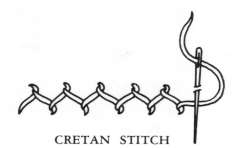

CRETAN STITCH

CRETAN STITCH

The Cretan stitch has the appearance of an open braid. Different effects can be achieved when Cretan stitches are worked close together, far apart, straight, or slanted. This stitch is most often used for oblong spaces or borders.

FEATHER STITCH

This is the stitch most often used to outline the patches in crazy quilts. It also makes an excellent border stitch.

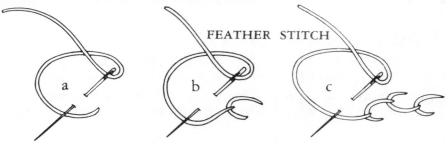

FEATHER STITCH

The *chain stitches* are economical stitches, using very little yarn on the back of the canvas. They are often used, therefore, as filling or background stitches to cover large surface areas.

CHAIN STITCH

To make a simple chain stitch, loop the thread under the needle as you draw it through.

LAZY DAISY STITCH

This is a detached chain stitch made by separating each stitch from the previous one.

CHAIN STITCH

LAZY DAISY STITCH

SEED STITCH

This tiny detached chain stitch is made by pulling the stitch up short.

VANDYKE STITCH

The Vandyke stitch creates a smooth braid down the center of your embroidery as you work from side to side across previously worked stitches. Different effects are created according to the size and proximity of the stitches. It is important to keep the tension even as you work.

Knot stitches have a rugged quality in contrast to the smoother background stitches. They stand out away from the background fabric.

BULLION STITCH

This stitch is made by wrapping the needle several times with the working thread before pushing it through the fabric. Different effects result from the number of times you wrap the needle. Long knots curl, making interesting flowers or animal fur. Short knots stay flat.

Don't confuse this stitch with bullion thread, a wire thread coiled like a spring.

ELONGATED FRENCH KNOT

This stitch appears to be on a stem. To execute it, bring the needle through to the face of the fabric and wrap the working thread once around the needle; next, keeping the thread taut, insert the needle about $\frac{1}{4}$ inch away from where you brought it through. The distance between the two points determines the length of the stem.

This stitch is very effectively used for flowers, when several stitches radiate from a center point, or for falling petals, when used singly.

SEED STITCH

VANDYKE STITCH

BULLION STITCH

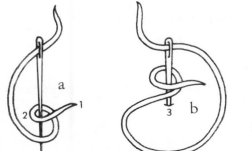

ELONGATED FRENCH KNOT

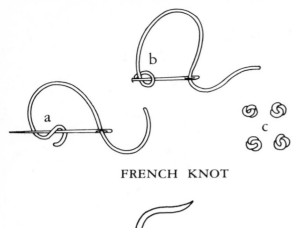

FRENCH KNOT

FRENCH KNOT

The size of the knot is determined by the thickness of the thread and the size of the needle. It is wise to wrap the working thread only once around the needle for neat, uniform results. These knots are most versatile. They can be worked close together for a full bodied effect or scattered for a more airy effect.

Detached stitches are detached from the background fabric. They are worked in various ways. When weaving these stitches, push the needle through the yarn eye first to avoid snagging your previous stitches.

RAISED CUP STITCH

The raised cup is a triangle of three stitches on which rows of woven loops are made to form a cup.

WHIPPED SPIDER WEB

Work spokes and whip the thread around each spoke. The spokes may be of equal length or different lengths. They may be tightly or loosely whipped for different effects.

RAISED CUP STITCH

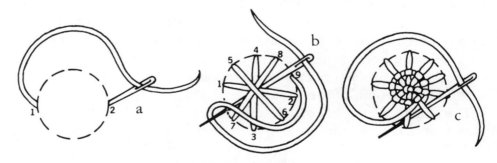

WHIPPED SPIDER WEB

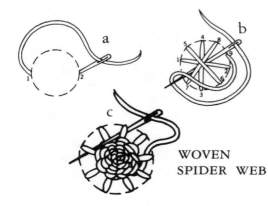

WOVEN SPIDER WEB

WOVEN SPIDER WEB

Weave the thread in and out of an uneven number of spokes to form the web.

Chapter Six
Introduction to Design

A design is as individual as the signature of the designer. Yet the effect of a design depends as much upon the observer as it does the designer since design elicits feelings and reactions. Design has a physical, emotional, and intellectual impact on us. One can needlepoint something physical (such as *Doll,* Color Plate C/D); one can stitch one's mood (such as *Joy,* Color Plate I/J); one can embroider a thought (such as *Rainbow,* Color Plate R). Thus needlery and the designs you choose become a language in themselves, a mode of communication. They often express thoughts and feelings in a manner far more personal and meaningful than words alone can.

History has been recorded for centuries through designs ranging from primitive cave paintings to extravagant gold work from Egyptian tombs. Ancient art forms, primitive as they are, teach us that the basics of design are instinctive to humans. The elements of design are echoed throughout nature; we have only to observe it. Upon close scrutiny, one discovers there are certain principals which can apply to all design.

Design Basics

A design is both visual and structural. What we see are the visual elements. The structural elements are what makes it work, what holds it together. A design may be functional, as a mechanical device, or it can be expressive, as in the visual arts. All these elements are interrelated in the definition of any given design. You as the designer choose these elements and decide upon the relationships among them and the roles they will play.

SPACE

The most basic element of design is space. All space, defined or undefined, focal point or background, becomes part of the overall design; and each space influences every other space. The relationship of these areas defines the scale of your design. Do not neglect the background space; its color, texture, and character will affect the entire piece.

CONTOUR

Straight or curved lines are the skeletal structure from which shapes are formed. Line is the structure upon which design is built. Line is the most basic and also the most abstract form of expression known, whether in the stick figures of cave paintings or the sophisticated structure of Mondrian paintings.

Shapes can be geometric, natural, abstract, or unintended. The latter shapes are happenings, not representative of anything other than their own movement, coming about, perhaps, by an exciting array or arrangement of tones.

CONTRAST

The differences between light and dark tones allow us to see form. The stronger the contrast, the stronger the form.

TEXTURE

The sensual element of design is texture. Tactile textures are those which can be felt, like roughness or smoothness. Visual textures are those which can be seen, like flatness or shininess. The contrasts in textures are as strong as those in colors, but we are often less aware of them. The same color may appear as two distinct colors in different textures. Texture is often used subtly, and its very subtlety is one of its strongest characteristics.

COLOR

Color is a great plaything and like other playthings, the more one knows about it, the more pleasure one can derive from it. Color is a force; it is based on contrasts and similarities. Color can be a force of movement in a design since the effects of colors working together can vary from one area of the design to another. Plan all your colors from the start, for they all affect one another. Color decisions are personal; you may understand intellectually the characteristics of color, but the best color tool you can have is knowing yourself well. Know your likes and dislikes, be aware of your reactions. Do not follow color fads; they will pass. Your personal preferences and emotional reactions might change at times, but throughout, they are yours alone.

A color wheel best displays color characteristics and relationships. Red, yellow, and blue are pure, primary colors. All other colors are created from mixtures of these. Orange, green, and violet are secondary colors—created by mixing two primary colors in equal proportions. The tertiary colors, created by mixing a primary color and one of its secondary colors, are red-violet, blue-violet, blue-green, yellow-green, yellow-orange, and red-orange.

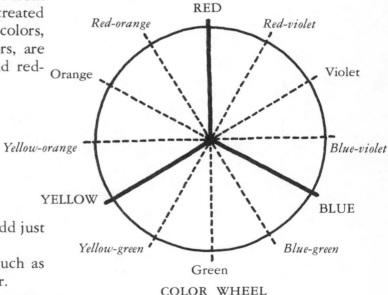

COLOR WHEEL

color harmonies

Certain color schemes, called harmonies, can please the eye and add just the right visual element to your design.

Complementary colors are those opposite on the color wheel, such as blue and orange. Complementary colors tend to intensify each other.

Analogous colors are adjacent, for example, blue, blue-green, and green. An analogous harmony can be the unifying element in a design.

Monochromatic colors are different values or intensities of the same color, for example, dark green, green, and light green. A monochromatic harmony can have a soothing, smooth effect.

hue

The term *hue* refers to colors that have no black or white mixed in them. (A color or hue plus black produces a *shade*; a color or hue plus white produces a *tint*.)

intensity

A color may be strong or soft, intense or dull. To make a color less intense (duller), mix it with a complementary color. Red mixed into green, for example, becomes a muddy color. Most of the time certain colors must be subordinate to others to achieve balance.

value

Value is the lightness or darkness of a color. A monochromatic color scheme is an example of different values of the same color. The stronger the contrast in value, the more powerful the impact.

SHADING

Look at the subject of your design in its natural environment. Where is it darker, where lighter? Realistic shading can be achieved through color or texture or a combination of the two. Don't hesitate to experiment. Many complex images can be derived through shading by a few simple changes in color or texture or scale.

If you are working a landscape design, work the foreground in darker tones and the background in lighter tones to give the illusion of distance. The same rules apply to both painting and needlework. To give the illusion of a curved surface or a three-dimensional effect, make the outer edges darker. Use at least three shades of the same color.

BALANCE

Good design is a plan for order and unity, a composition. The relationships that define balance and unity in a design are simultaneously structural and visual; the potentials and limitations of space, the position of the shapes and forms, the differences of texture, and the hue, intensity, and value of the chosen colors are all involved. You must create the balance of the structural and visual elements that is right for your design.

Design Sources

Everywhere! Nature itself is a miracle in design. For centuries flora and fauna have inspired man to artistic heights. Architecture, with its balance and interplay of geometrics and patterns is an excellent design source. Museums offer a wealth of ideas, as does history itself. A personal reflection often inspires motifs: your home, pets, sports, school, travels, an anniversary, a birthday. Children are a surprising source of design—their candid comments, their joyful paintings, their honest and fresh outlook on life. Whimsy is always welcome; the greatest gift of all may be a spontaneous smile!

The Recommended Approach

- Be simple in your endeavors. Remember simple sophistication?

- You are not only a designer, you are an interpreter, for you must translate your idea into stitchery, at once a challenge and a joy!

- Before you begin, ask yourself: What is the purpose of this project? Is it decorative or functional? Will it receive a lot of wear? What size will it be?

Design Techniques

Shape your idea into a design. Think about the visual and structural elements of design (see page 51). Make a drawing. Experiment with space, contour, color.

Experiment with yarn colors and textures. The materials become an integral part of the design. Decide which stitches will work best. Make a small sample swatch (see page 21).

Choose the working techniques that best suit your design. It is wise to start with one you know, but allow yourself the freedom to change, expand, interpret as you work.

Think free, be all you can be!

If your tastes be contemporary or traditional,
     casual or elegant,
     simple or sophisticated . . . this book is for you.

Why not love it all?
Casual elegance and *simple sophistication!*

Think of yourself in terms of growth, movement, change, and challenge—rather than traditional categories and boundaries. Rules are not there to be broken; they are there as a structure on which to grow and build your own world. Don't be a spectator, be an adventurer; for what you see is also what you feel, what you think.

Go to it. . . . Take the ground rules
     Sharpen them with experience
     Stretch them with experimentation
     and make them work for you
     with curiosity, confidence, and courage.

PART TWO
Needlery Designs

In this part of the book there are twenty-six needlery designs, one for each letter of the alphabet. They are quite diverse in feeling and in purpose. Some are useful; some are purely decorative; some are just for fun and whimsy.

Thumb through the color plates and see which designs strike your fancy and suit your taste. The instructions for each are thorough and easy to follow, from step one through finishing. Refer to Part One, Needlery Basics, for explanations of technical terms.

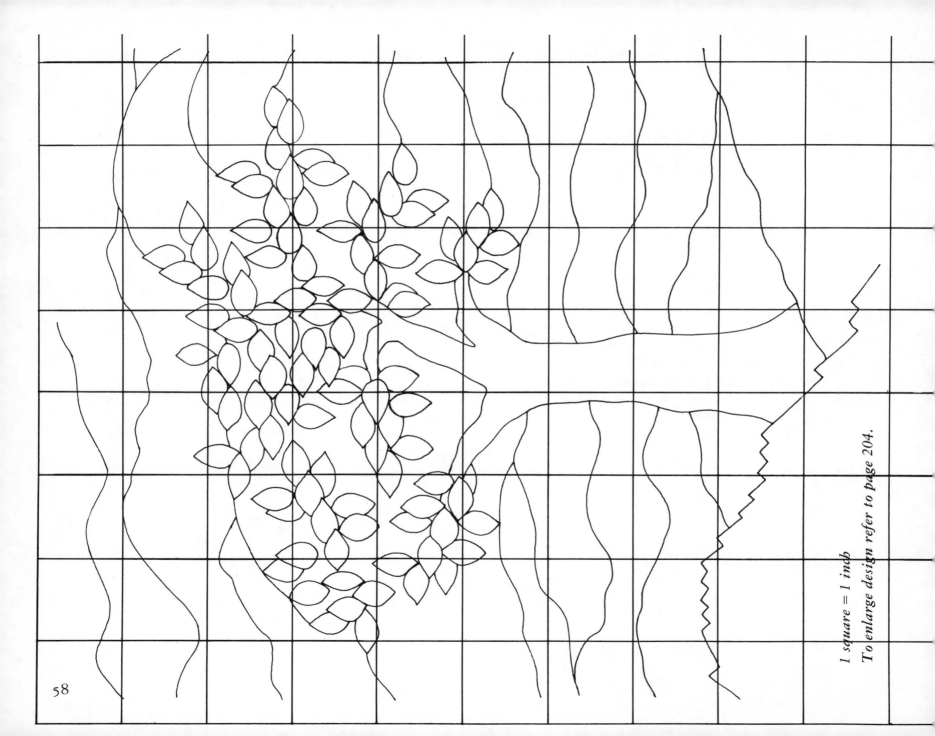

58

1 square = 1 inch

To enlarge design refer to page 204.

Album

DEXTERITY: Level III

MATERIALS

Tapestry needle #20
Mono canvas #18, cut 9½ by 11½ inches
Photo album with needlework insert
DMC Perle cotton, #3 weight
DMC Mouline cotton embroidery floss

DESIGN AREA	STITCHES	PERLE COTTON	
		Amount	*Color*
Tree trunk	Brick stitch	1 skein	#938 brown
Tree leaves	Leaf stitch	1 skein	#937 green
		1 skein	#470 green
		1 skein	#471 green
		1 skein	#472 green
Right hill	French knots	*	#937 green
		*	#470 green
		*	#471 green
		*	#472 green

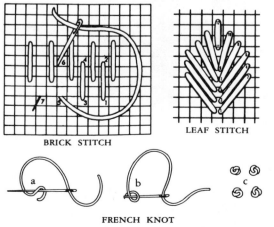

BRICK STITCH

LEAF STITCH

FRENCH KNOT

BARGELLO RHYTHM —LEFT HILL

BULLION STITCH

LOOP STITCH

GOBELIN STITCH

ENCROACHING GOBELIN

			FLOSS
		1 skein	#353 salmon
		1 skein	#351 coral
		1 skein	# 43 yellow
			PERLE COTTON
Left hill	Bargello	*	#472 green
		*	#937 green
		*	#470 green
			FLOSS
Cabbage	Bullion stitch	1 skein	#902 garnet
Cauliflower	French knots	1 skein	#822 white
Lettuce	Loop stitch	1 skein	#996 green
			PERLE COTTON
Center hill	Encroaching Gobelin stitch	1 skein	#471 green
Sky	Straight Gobelin stitch	1 skein	#415 grey
		2 skeins	#932 blue
		2 skeins	#800 blue
Cloud	Straight Gobelin stitch	1 skein	ecru

* Use remainder of yarn from other design areas.

SPECIAL HINTS

It is advisable to use a working frame to avoid pulling the canvas out of shape while working long Gobelin stitches. Frames are available at art supply stores or through mail-order catalogs. Trace the design directly onto the canvas with pale-grey indelible felt-tip pen.

Finished piece is 10¼ inches wide and 11½ inches high.

INSTRUCTIONS
tree trunk

Use a single strand of #938 brown Perle cotton, approximately 18 inches long. Work in brick stitch over three threads. Follow the outline of the tree trunk, working the rows back and forth. Use half stitches where necessary to conform to the outline.

tree leaves

Use a single strand of #937 dark green, then two medium shades, #470 and #471 green, and then #472 light green. Start at the lower right branch, then work the left branch. Work the center leaves last so the stitches can build on one another. Stitch the whole leaves first, then do the partial ones. Although the precise color pattern does not matter, there should be a balance of light and dark tones.

right hill

To create a field of flowers, first work French knots in a single strand of the four shades of leaf-green Perle cotton #3. Scatter French knots at random, catching one canvas thread at a time. Fill in with additional knots, using in turn a double strand of floss in salmon, coral, and yellow, until the entire hill area is covered with French knots.

left hill

Start at the top and work down. Use a single strand of Perle Cotton #3, and work a bargello stitch over three threads with a step of one. Work one row of light green, one of dark, and one of medium two times. Then work one light, one medium, and one dark; then one medium and one light; and finish the last row with medium green for the background. Use the dark bargello rows for placement of cabbage, cauliflowers, and lettuce.

Five heads of cabbage on the bottom row of dark bargello: Use a full six strands of DMC floss #902, and work bullion stitches. Wrap the needle seven times for the two center leaves, twelve times for the next two leaves, twenty times for the two outer leaves. Curve the stitches slightly to create a cabbage shape.

Five heads of cauliflower on the next row of dark bargello: Use a full six strands of DMC floss #822, and make French knots. Stitch eighteen knots for each head of cauliflower and mass the stitches close together to form the heads.

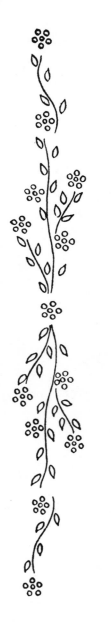

Three heads of lettuce on the top row of dark bargello: Use a full six strands of DMC floss #996, and work a loop stitch. Make a small loop on the surface of the canvas, and hold it in place by a small flat stitch on the back of the canvas. Group ten loop stitches together to create a lettuce shape.

center hill

Use a single strand of Perle cotton #3 green #471, and make an encroaching Gobelin stitch. Start at the top of the hill and follow the outline, stepping up or down one thread when necessary to retain the shape of the hill. Using the first row across the top as a guide, continue working back and forth until the area is filled. It may be necessary to use half stitches to conform to other hills.

sky and cloud

Use a single strand of Perle cotton, medium blue #932, and make a straight Gobelin stitch. Start at the inside of the tree branches and work toward the outer edge of the canvas. Follow the outlines for each row. Work the light-blue (#800) sky from the tree trunk to the outer edge. Work the ecru clouds, and the grey (#415) sky in the same manner, from inner canvas to outer edge.

FINISHING

When a working frame is used, blocking should not be necessary. Remove the canvas from the frame, fold the top raw canvas edge under, and press with a steam iron to insure a fold. Fold the two sides of raw canvas under and press. Fold and press the bottom edge last. Slide the needlework into the photo album cover.

Variations on a Theme

The needlework album insert can be a birth announcement if you embroider dates and data in the clouds. With the addition of embroidered names among the leaves of the tree and an appropriate frame, the album can become a family tree. (See graphed alphabets, pages 119 and 165, and numerals, page 165.)

Butterfly

DEXTERITY: Level I

MATERIALS

Tapestry needle #22
Hardware screen, 4 by 5 inches, 16 mesh
Frame, 5½ by 6½ inches
Mirror for backing, 5 by 6 inches
Pearsall's Filo-Floss six-strand silk

| DESIGN AREA | STITCHES | YARN | |
		Amount	Color
Body	Straight Gobelin stitch	1 skein	#601 grey
Head	Straight Gobelin stitch	1 skein	#178 black
Wings	Continental stitch	1 skein	# 93 brown
		1 skein	#156 gold
		1 skein	#91B cream
		1 skein	# 99 wine
Wing markings	French knots	*	# 99 wine
Antennae		*	#178 black

* Use remainder of yarn from other design areas.

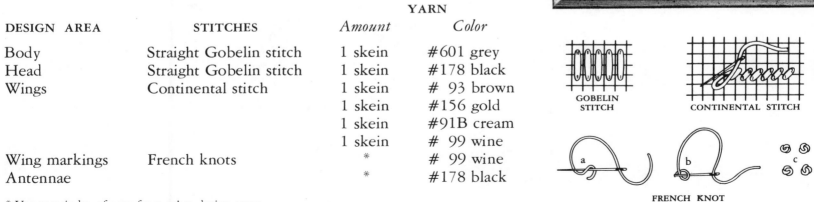

GOBELIN STITCH

CONTINENTAL STITCH

FRENCH KNOT

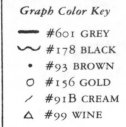

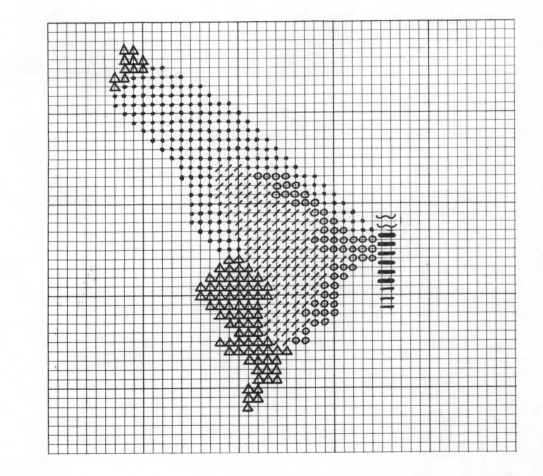

Butterfly, page 63

Chair, page 91   Doll, page 95

Eagle, page 100

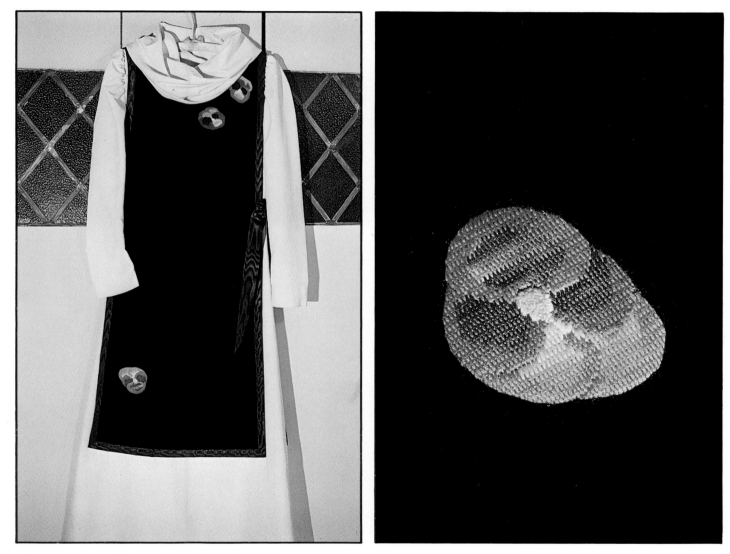

Girl, page 109

Heart, page 114

Initials, page 117   *Joy, page 122*

King, page 125

Love, page 129

Mirror, page 133

Nautilus, page 136

Ocean, page 140

Pillow, page 144

Quilt, page 148

80

Rainbow, page 166

Thistle, page 173

Vest, page 179

Weathervane, page 185

Xmas, page 188

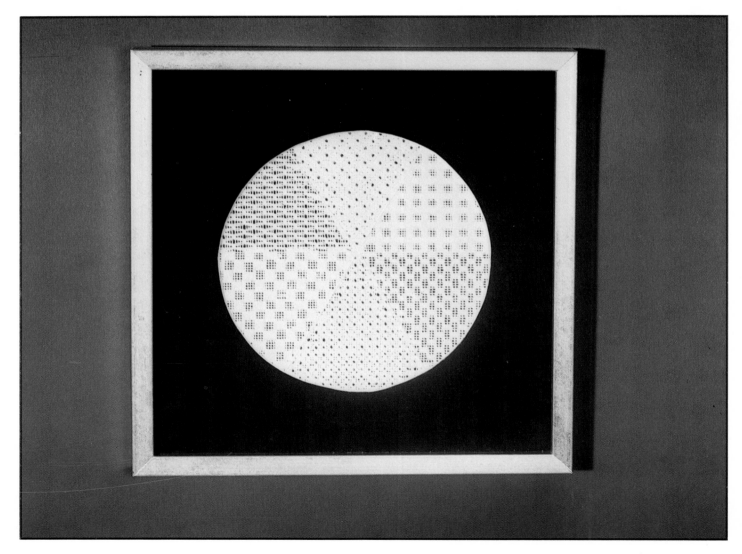

Zodiac, page 198

SPECIAL HINTS

Cover the raw edges of the screen with masking tape. Handle the silk yarn carefully as it frays easily, and use short strands, no more than 12 inches long. You may wish to run the yarn through beeswax for ease in handling.

Finished piece is 6½ inches wide and 5½ inches high.

INSTRUCTIONS

body

Use the full six strands of Pearsall's silk #601 grey, and work a straight Gobelin stitch horizontally over two wire threads. Start twenty-seven holes from the top and forty-seven holes from either side of the raw screen edge. Work down ten holes. Repeat the entire body twice; then work the center portion of the body a third time for a more realistic, rounded effect.

head

Use the full six strands of Pearsall's silk #178 black, and work a straight Gobelin stitch over two wire threads. Repeat several times at the top of body, through the same holes, to create a roundness.

wings

Use the full six strands of Pearsall's silk #93 brown, and work a continental stitch. Start at the first row of the body, and work to the top of the wing, in accordance with the graph. Then work #156 gold, #91(B) cream, and #99 wine in the same manner.

wing markings

Use two strands of Pearsall's silk #99 wine, and make French knots. Work six knots for small, nine knots for medium, twelve knots for large markings at the wingtips.

antennae

Use two strands of Pearsall's silk #178 black. Run the needle through the back of the body and out the top of the head. Position the needle in

the hole at the end of the antennae; wrap the yarn around one wire, and tie a single knot. Cut the yarn close to the knot on the back side of the needlework, and secure with white glue.

FINISHING:

Remove the masking tape from the screen edges (or it will reflect in the mirror), and glue the raw edges of the screen to the inner lip of the front of the frame. Glue the wispy silk ends onto the back of needlework for a flat finish (since the back side will reflect in the mirror). Glue the mirror onto the back of the frame.

Variations on a Theme

The small needlework butterfly can be worked in a variety of colors on a decorative (non-functional) fireplace screen or on a well protected front door screen.

Chair

DEXTERITY: Level II

MATERIALS

Tapestry needle #20
Mono canvas #12, 8 by 10 inches
Wooden-chair kit, with seat 7 inches wide, 6½ inches deep, 12 inches
    high
Paternayan Persian 3-ply wool
Penelope crewel wool

DESIGN AREA	STITCHES	PERSIAN YARN	
		Amount	*Color*
Heart	Bargello stitch	3 strands	#860 pink
Background	Brick stitch	42 strands	#012 white
		CREWEL YARN	
Vine	Threaded running stitch	4 strands	#594 light green

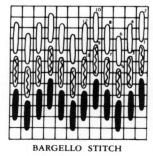

BARGELLO STITCH

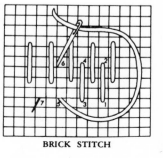

BRICK STITCH

THREADED RUNNING STITCH

LAZY DAISY STITCH

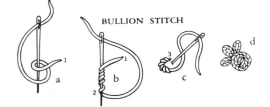

BULLION STITCH

Leaves	Lazy daisy stitch	4 strands	#595 dark green
Rose buds	Lazy daisy stitch	2 strands	#551 light rose
Rose	Bullion stitch	*	#551 light rose
		2 strands	#553 dark rose

* Use remainder of yarn from other design areas.

SPECIAL HINTS

Center the seat of the chair over the canvas, and mark the outline of the seat. Work ½ inch beyond this outline to allow for the thickness of the seat. It is needless to outline the vine pattern since the background stitches will cover your lines. Placement of the design does not have to be exact. Use the graph as a guide for the approximate placement of the heart and vines to be embroidered.

Finished needlework piece is 5½ inches wide and 6¼ inches deep.

INSTRUCTIONS

heart

Use a full three strands of Paternayan #860 pink, and work a bargello stitch in the following rhythm: over four threads with a step of two threads, to conform to the heart shape. Use a half stitch where indicated on the graph. Begin the heart twenty canvas threads from the center bottom.

background

Use two strands of Paternayan #012 white, and work a brick stitch over four threads. Begin at the top center of the heart and work to ½ inch beyond the edge of the seat line to allow for turning under the cushion. Use a half stitch where necessary to conform to the heart shape.

vine

Use one strand of Penelope #594 light green, and make a threaded running stitch. Use the graph as a guide for approximate placement.

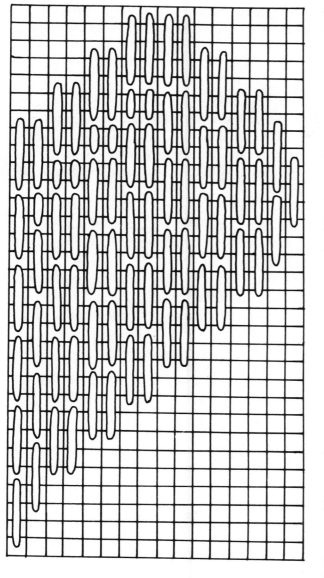

BARGELLO RHYTHM FOR HEART

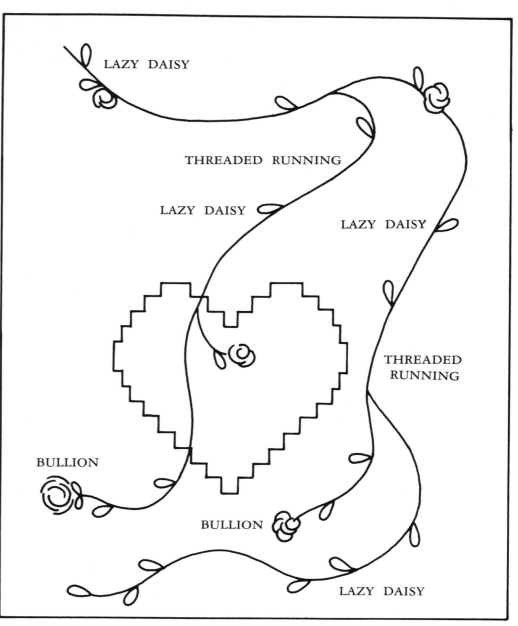

LAZY DAISY

THREADED RUNNING

LAZY DAISY

LAZY DAISY

THREADED RUNNING

BULLION

BULLION

LAZY DAISY

Actual size

You may wish to place the design by basting with cotton thread first, and then work the embroidery. Be sure to remove the cotton thread upon completion.

leaves

Use one strand of Penelope #595 dark green, and make a lazy daisy stitch. Place leaves at random, using the graph as a guide. Work a single stitch for small leaves, a double stitch for medium leaves, and a triple stitch for large leaves, making each stitch over your original stitch and slightly larger. Add one green bullion stitch to each small bullion rose.

roses

For the buds, use one strand of Penelope #551 light rose, and work a tight lazy daisy stitch. For the flowers, use one strand of Penelope #551 light rose for the center petals, and one strand of Penelope #553 dark rose for the outer petals. Bullion stitches curled around one another will create the rose shape—three stitches for the center, four stitches for the outer petals. Wrap your needle six times for the center stitches, and ten times for the outer stitches.

FINISHING

Wrap the canvas around the seat, and staple it in place. Glue the felt to the seat bottom, and screw the seat to the chair.

VARIATIONS ON A THEME

The heart and flower design of the doll's chair can be used as a cover for a brick door stop. Trace the outline of the brick to make sure the canvas is the proper size and enlarge the background where necessary.

Doll

DEXTERITY: Level I

MATERIALS

Tapestry needle #20
Mono canvas #10, 14 by 14 inches
Calico: blue, yellow, and green scraps, approximately 8 inches square,
    for the back of the doll
Polyester fiberfill for stuffing
Balsam or potpourri for stuffing (optional)
Fawcett linen, 10/5 weight
DMC Mouline cotton embroidery floss

		LINEN YARN	
DESIGN AREA	STITCHES	*Amount*	*Color*
Face	Continental stitch	1 skein	peach
Babushka	Continental stitch	1 skein	blue
Dots	French knots	1 skein	white
Blouse	Continental stitch	1 skein	maize
		1 skein	light blue

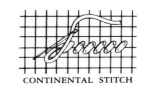

CONTINENTAL STITCH

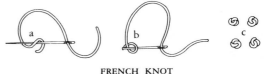

FRENCH KNOT

GOBELIN
STITCH

CROSS-STITCH

LOOP STITCH

SATIN STITCH

Apron			
Background	Continental stitch	*	white
Waistband	Continental stitch	*	pink
Small hearts	Straight Gobelin stitch	*	pink
Large heart	Straight Gobelin stitch	*	cherry
Skirt			
Background	Continental stitch	1 skein	green
Floral design	Continental stitch	1 skein	cherry
		1 skein	pink

COTTON EMBROIDERY FLOSS

Skirt Xs	Cross-stitch	1 skein	#744 yellow
Hair	Loop stitch	2 skeins	#938 brown
Eye lashes	Straight stitch	*	#938 brown
Mouth	Satin stitch	1 skein	#815 red
Eyes	Satin stitch	1 skein	#311 blue
Nose	French knots	*	#815 red

* Use remainder of yarn from other design areas.

SPECIAL HINTS

Trace the outline of the design directly onto the canvas. The use of a working frame will prevent the continental stitches from pulling the canvas out of shape. Linen yarn has a natural striation within the fiber. This adds to the rustic charm, and should not be considered a defect.

Finished doll is 10 inches high and 7 inches wide at the widest point.

INSTRUCTIONS
face and babushka

Use a single strand of linen, and work a continental stitch—the face first, in peach, followed by the babushka, in blue.

blouse

Use a single strand of linen, and work a continental stitch—the background in maize and the stripes in light blue.

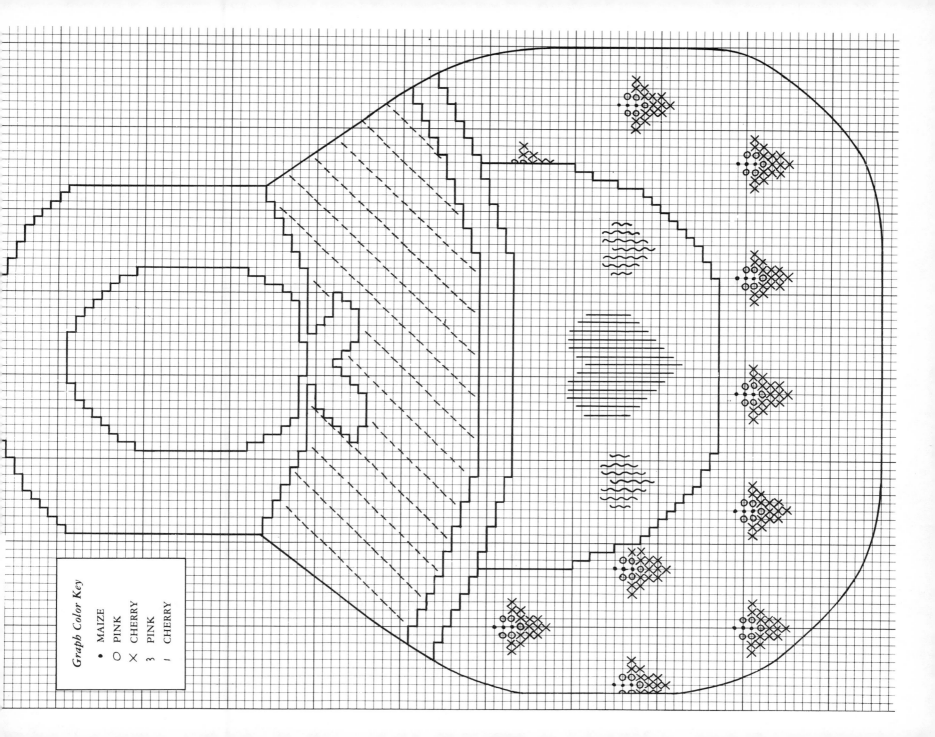

Graph Color Key

- MAIZE
○ PINK
✕ CHERRY
₹ PINK
╱ CHERRY

apron

Use a single strand of linen, and work a straight Gobelin stitch for the hearts—the large heart in cherry, the small hearts in pink. Finish the apron background with continental stitches in white; use pink for the waistband.

skirt

Use a single strand of linen and work a continental stitch. Following the graph, work the flowers first, then fill in the background with dark green.

embroidery details

Use a single strand of white linen, and make French knots to create polka dots on the babushka; place them at random. Use a full six strands of DMC floss, #744 yellow, and work cross-stitches on the skirt. Place them three spaces apart, every two rows.

hair

Use a full strand of DMC floss, #938 brown, and make a loop stitch on the front of the canvas; follow this with a small flat stitch on the back. Stitch small loops on either side of the face for the curls; work larger loops at the forehead for bangs.

braids

Cut twelve strands of floss, each 9 inches long. Fold the strands in half; tie at the center with one additional 9-inch strand. To braid, divide the floss into three sections, eight strands each and braid. To end, tie at the bottom with one 6-inch strand of cherry yarn, and make a bow.

eyelashes

Use the same brown yarn, and small straight stitches.

nose

Use a full strand of DMC #815 red, and make two French knots.

mouth
Work in DMC #815 red, and make satin stitches for the desired shape.

eyes
Use a full six strands of DMC #311 blue, and work satin stitches many times over, to make the eyes round.

FINISHING
Remove the needlework from the working frame, and block in the traditional manner. Trim the excess raw canvas to within ½ inch of the needlework.

calico backing
Using the outline of the canvas as a pattern, trace the skirt area onto the green calico, the blouse area onto the yellow calico, the babushka onto the blue calico (with a point at the back as illustrated). Adding ¼-inch seams all around the edges, cut out the calico. Stitch the blouse and skirt together with a ¼-inch seam. Press the point of the babushka ¼ inch under, and use blind stitches to attach it to the blouse. Place right sides together. Stitch the canvas to the calico, matching the seams carefully. Leave the bottom edge open.

Stitch as close to the needlework as possible. Trim the seam excess, and clip the curves. Turn the right side out, and press the seams flat with your fingers. Stuff with fiberfill till firm. Balsam or potpourri can be used as a partial stuffing for a fragrant result. Close the bottom opening with slip stitches.

VARIATIONS ON A THEME
The doll becomes a very personal toy when you add a child's name or initials to the apron. Use one of the needlepoint alphabets included in the book (pages 119 and 165). You can change the hair style and color to match the child's.

DEXTERITY: Level III

MATERIALS

Tapestry needle #22

Mono canvas #18, 11 by 13 inches

Weathered wood for frame: two pieces, approximately 12 by 2 inches; two pieces, approximately 10 by 2 inches

Branches for shadow effect

Plywood, $\frac{1}{4}$ inch thick, 9 by 11 inches

Springer Bella Donna rayon

Paternayan Persian 3-ply wool

DESIGN AREA	STITCHES	RAYON YARN	
		Amount	*Color*
Eagle	Encroaching Gobelin stitch	2 skeins	#841 brown
Beak	Continental stitch		#841 brown
		PERSIAN YARN	
Sun	Continental stitch	7 strands	#444 apricot
Sky/from top to sun	Encroaching Gobelin stitch	6 strands	#G37 pale green

ENCROACHING GOBELIN

CONTINENTAL STITCH

		2 strands	#015 ecru
		6 strands	#437 pale yellow
		6 strands	#467 yellow
		2 strands	#442 lemon
Sky/left side	Encroaching Gobelin stitch	1 strand	#265 pink
		2 strands	#464 extra pale pink
		3 strands	#454 pale apricot
		3 strands	#444 apricot
		1 strand	#430 dusty pink
		1 strand	#R78 peach
		*	#454 pale apricot
		1 strand	#138 pale beige
		1 strand	#166 grey
		1 strand	#392 silver grey
Sky/right side	Encroaching Gobelin stitch	8 strands	#457 pale gold
		3 strands	#447 gold
		3 strands	#427 dark gold
		3 strands	#424 orange
		2 strands	#225 rust
		2 strands	#210 umber
		2 strands	#843 coral
		3 strands	#278 pale umber
		3 strands	#254 lavender
		1 strand	#855 rose
		2 strands	#265 pink
		2 strands	#444 apricot
		1 strand	#138 light beige
		1 strand	#133 beige
		1 strand	#166 grey
		1 strand	#392 silver grey

* Use remainder of yarn from other design areas.

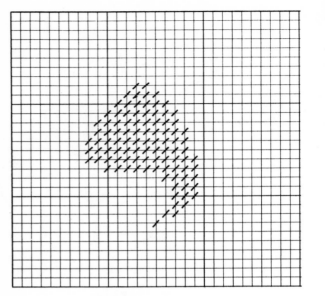

GRAPH FOR BEAK

SPECIAL HINTS

Trace the outline of the eagle and the sun onto the canvas. It is advisable to use a working frame for stitching since the encroaching Gobelin stitch tends to pull the canvas out of shape.

Finished piece is $10\frac{1}{2}$ inches wide and $11\frac{1}{2}$ inches high.

INSTRUCTIONS

eagle

You may wish to color the canvas in the eagle area since the slanted stitches tend to expose the canvas. Use a single strand of Springer Bella Donna #841 brown, and work a continental stitch for the beak. Following the graph, start at the point of the beak and work toward the head. Use the same yarn for the eagle's body and work an encroaching Gobelin stitch over four threads. Start at the top and work down; use a half stitch where necessary to conform to the outline and add to the feather effect.

sun

Use a single strand of Paternayan #444 apricot, separated from one 3-ply strand, and work a continental stitch in rows to conform to the sun's outline and the eagle's silhouette.

sky

Using a single strand of Paternayan yarn separated from one 3-ply strand, work an encroaching Gobelin stitch over four threads. The shadings in the sky do not have to be precise. For a natural effect, each row should blend into the next. Use Color Plate E as a guide; then use the colors in a paint-stroke fashion for a striated sky. Follow the yarn chart, working from top to bottom.

FINISHING

Remove the canvas from the working frame to block.

Center the canvas on the $\frac{1}{4}$-inch plywood (9 by 11 inches). Turn under the raw edges and staple the canvas in place.

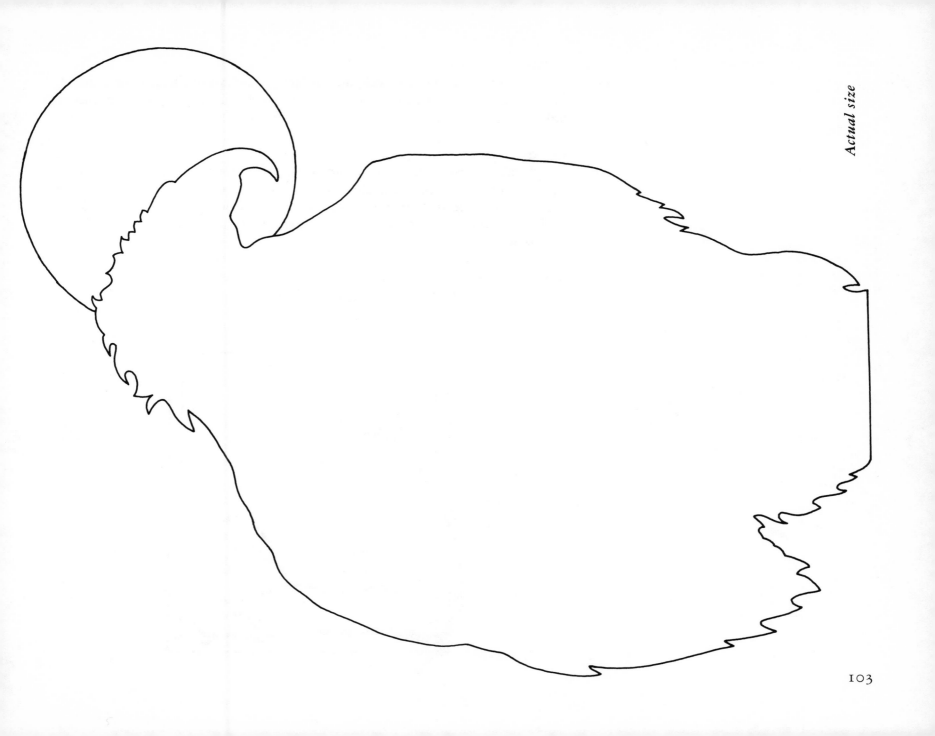

frame

Use the weathered wood and cut four sides. An old fruit crate is ideal; driftwood or scraps from the local lumber yard, such as rough hewn plaster lath, can also be used. Overlap to form a frame, and nail in place.

talons

Bend two pipe cleaners to form feet. Wrap them with a single strand of Paternayan #447 gold, and glue the raw ends. Place the talons on the tree branch, and glue in a proper position for the eagle's silhouette. Additional branches can be glued to the edge of the frame for interesting shadow effects on the needlework.

VARIATIONS ON A THEME

Add a few hooks to the eagle's driftwood frame to make a handsome key or calendar holder.

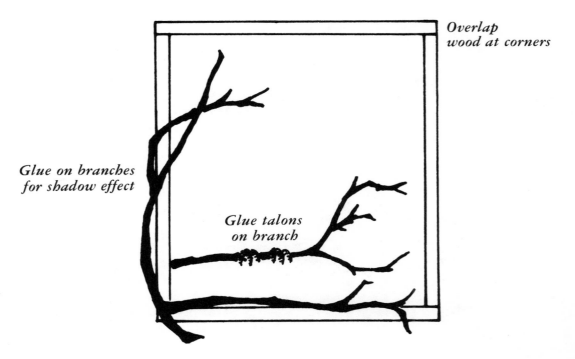

Overlap wood at corners

Glue on branches for shadow effect

Glue talons on branch

Flowers

DEXTERITY: Level II

STITCHES
    Encroaching Gobelin stitch: flowers
    French knots: flower centers

MATERIALS
    Tapestry needle #22
    Mono canvas #18, 4 by 12 inches
    DMC Mouline embroidery floss

1 skein #977 gold	1 skein #108 yellow ombre
1 skein #347 red	1 skein #919 burnt umber
1 skein #921 umber	1 skein #327 purple
1 skein #938 brown	1 skein #102 purple ombre
1 skein #744 yellow	1 skein #712 white

    $1\frac{1}{4}$ yards velvet 45 inches wide
    $1\frac{1}{4}$ yards lining 45 inches wide
    3 yards ribbon ties $1\frac{1}{2}''$ wide
    $5\frac{1}{4}$ yards ribbon trim $1\frac{1}{2}$ inches wide

ENCROACHING GOBELIN

Work this stitch over three threads instead of four

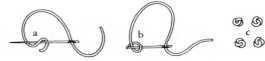

FRENCH KNOT

SPECIAL HINTS

Trace the outline of the flowers directly onto the canvas.
Finished tabard is 14 inches wide and 39 inches long.

INSTRUCTIONS

petals

Use a full 6 strands of floss and work an encroaching Gobelin stitch over three threads. Follow the illustration for a color guide. Work the inner colors first.

center

Use a full 6 strands of floss and work French knots. Work two layers of knots for fullness.

cutting out the tabard

Cut two rectangles 14 inches by 39 inches for the tabard. For the neckline, mark a point 2 inches in from the top corners, $2\frac{1}{4}$ inches down at center back, $3\frac{1}{2}$ inches down at center front. Draw a curved line between these points to form the neckline; cut out along the curve. Repeat the procedure for the lining.

appliqué

The technique used is reverse appliqué. Trim the excess canvas to within $\frac{1}{4}$ inch of the flower edges. Stay stitch two times—once around the canvas edge and once around the needlework edge. On the fabric front, pin the needlework in place. Lightly trace the outline of the raw canvas edge of the flowers with chalk. Unpin the flowers. Draw another outline $\frac{1}{2}$ inch inside the chalk outline; cut out the fabric around this second line. Clip $\frac{1}{8}$ inch around the opening. Place the flowers in the back of the opening (face side up); pin in place. Turn the raw fabric edge under all around the face of the flower; do not expose any raw canvas;

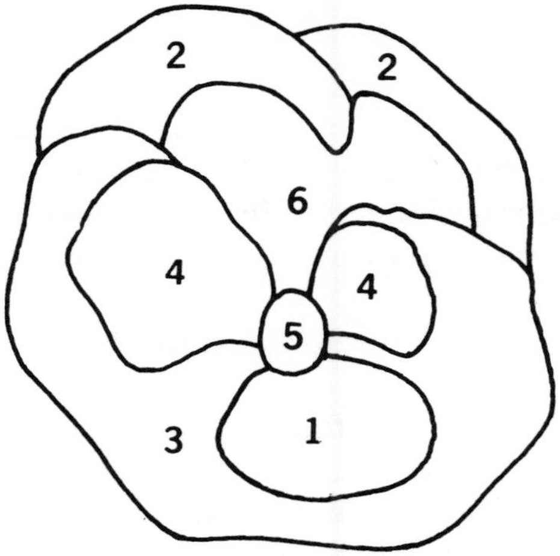

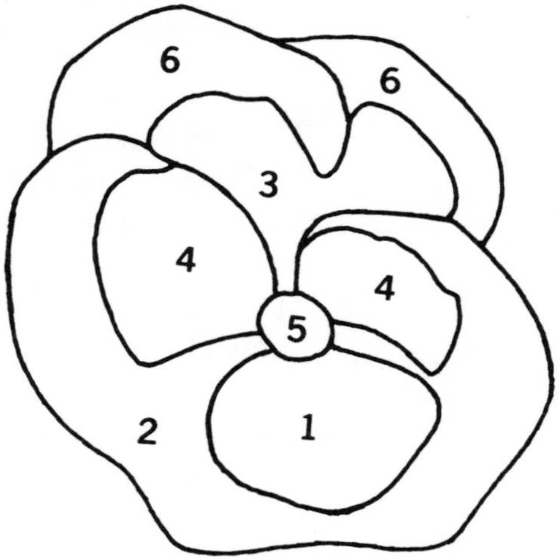

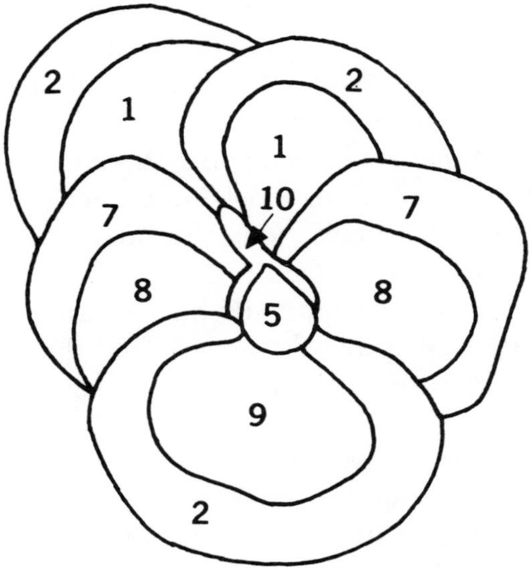

Color Key

1 #108 YELLOW OMBRE
2 #921 UMBER
3 #347 RED
4 #938 BROWN
5 #744 YELLOW
6 #977 GOLD
7 #919 BURNT UMBER
8 #327 PURPLE
9 #102 PURPLE OMBRE
10 #712 WHITE

Actual size

baste in place. Use a matching thread and a blind stitch to sew around the hole. Place the fabric face side down on a terry towel and gently steam the appliquéd areas.

FINISHING

With right sides together, pin the neckline of the front to the lining. Sew it in place to within $\frac{1}{2}$ inch of the raw shoulder edge. Clip the curves, turn the front right side out, and steam on a terry towel (do not press velvet). Repeat the procedure for the back.

With right sides together, sew the velvet front to the velvet back tapering slightly toward the shoulders. Turn right sides out and hemstitch the lining in place. With the tabard right side out, pin and baste the front to the lining, down both sides and $\frac{1}{4}$ inch in from the edge.

Try on the tabard. Pin four 27-inch ribbon ties in the desired place (below bustline, or at waistline or hipline), and tie them in place. Check the hemline, and cut the tabard to the desired length. Take off the tabard, and baste the hemlines as you did on the sides. Sew the ribbon ties in place.

Iron the remainder of the ribbon in half lengthwise. On the lining side, pin the ribbon along the basted line (slightly overlapping), and machine stitch it in place with matching thread.

Start at the lower left-hand corner of the hem and sew all of one side, across the front hem, along the other side, and across the back. Miter the corners, and pin the fold in place.

When the machine stitching is complete, return to these corners and secure them with blind stitches. Fold the ribbon toward the outside (velvet side) and secure with blind stitches, mitering the front corners.

VARIATIONS ON A THEME

The needlework pansies can be made into sachets or quaint pin cushions. Simply trace the outline onto backing fabric, cut out the shape allowing a $\frac{1}{4}$-inch seam, and stitch together leaving a small opening. Turn right side out, stuff with potpourri or cotton, then blind stitch closed.

Girl

DEXTERITY: Level II

MATERIALS

    Tapestry needle #20
    Mono canvas #10, 10 by 12 inches
    Wicker basket or frame, 8 by 10 inches
    Fawcett linen, 10/5 weight

DESIGN AREA	STITCHES	YARN Amount	Color
Clouds	French knots	2 skeins	white
Grass	Turkey work (cut)	2 skeins	spring green
Girl			
Hat	Continental stitch	1 skein	maize
Dress	Mosaic stitch	1 skein	pink
		1 skein	cherry
Hand/legs	Continental stitch	*	white
Shoes	Continental stitch	*	maize
Balloon	Satin stitch	*	pink
Sky	Encroaching Gobelin stitch	4 skeins	light blue

* Use remainder of yarn from other design areas.

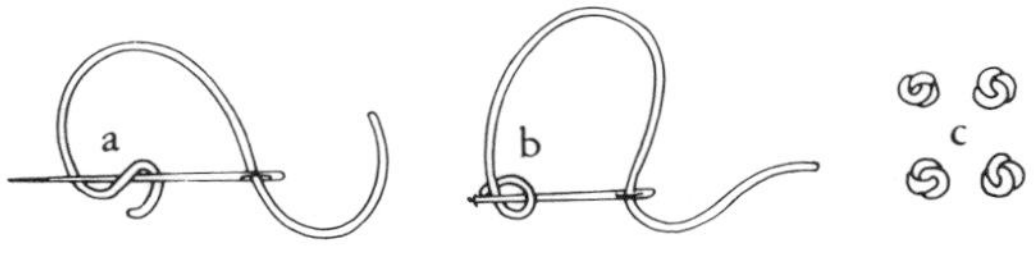

FRENCH KNOT

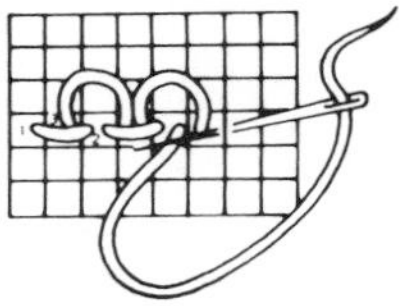

TURKEY WORK

CONTINENTAL STITCH

MOSAIC STITCH

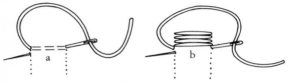

SATIN STITCH

ENCROACHING GOBELIN

*Work this stitch over three threads
instead of four*

SPECIAL HINTS

It is advisable to use a working frame since the encroaching Gobelin stitch pulls the canvas out of shape. Trace the design outlines directly onto the canvas. Linen yarn has a natural striation. This is not a defect; and it adds rustic charm to the needlework.

Finished piece is 10 inches wide and 8 inches high.

INSTRUCTIONS

clouds

Use a single strand of white, and make French knots, working the stitches in a random pattern rather than row by row to give a puffy effect. Fill in the cloud area, adding knots on top of knots for a dense effect.

hat and shoes

Use a single strand of maize, and work continental stitches, following the graph.

hand and legs

Use a single strand of white, and work continental stitches, following the graph.

dress

Use a single strand of pink and cherry. Work in mosaic stitches, alternating pink and cherry squares for a checkered effect.

balloon

Use a single strand of pink, and work satin stitches. Fill in the balloon area—first vertically, then a second time, diagonally, directly over the vertical stitches, for fullness.

sky

Use a single strand of light blue, and work encroaching Gobelin stitches over three threads from the top down; use a half stitch where necessary to conform to the design.

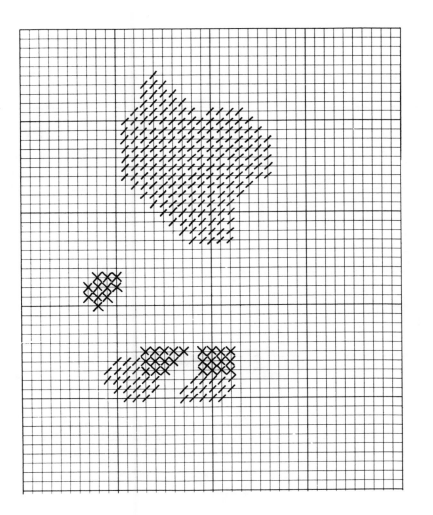

Graph Color Key

/ MAIZE

X WHITE

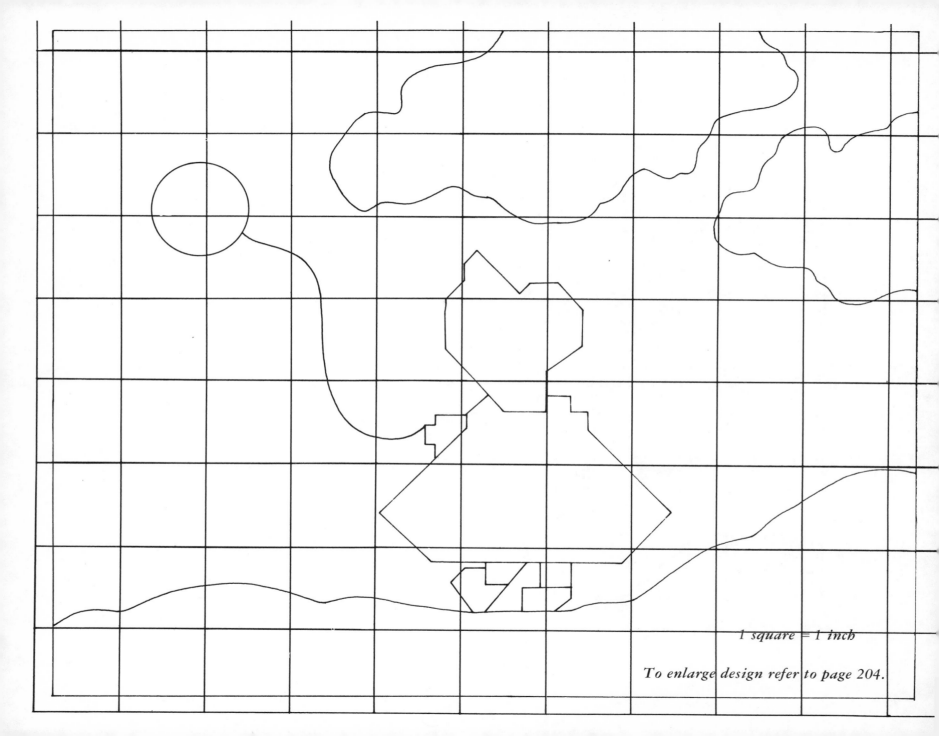

1 square = 1 inch

To enlarge design refer to page 204.

grass

Use a single strand of spring green and make turkey work stitches. Work from top to bottom, back and forth in rows; complete all the loop stitches before cutting.

FINISHING
balloon

Cut a maize strand 6 inches long. Bring the needle up at the hand, run the thread across the front of the canvas, and place the needle down at the base of the balloon. Secure with a few small stitches on the back of the canvas.

hat

Cut a cherry strand 6 inches long. Leave a tail on the front of the canvas; bring the needle down at the hat brim, across the back, and up at the opposite side. Tie a bow, and trim.

needlework piece

Remove the needlework from the frame and block in the traditional manner. Wrap it around the 8- by 10-inch plywood board, and staple it in place. Set it inside the 8- by 10-inch wicker basket for a shadow-box effect (or use any suitable frame).

VARIATIONS ON A THEME

The little girl makes a charming room sign for a real-life little girl's room. It can be a birth announcement if you add embroidered lettering. (See graphed alphabets, pages 119 and 165, and numerals, page 165.)

Heart

DEXTERITY: Level I

STITCHES

Bargello stitch: background
Bullion stitch: flower, leaves

MATERIALS

Tapestry needle #22
Mono canvas #18, 12 by 12 inches
$\frac{1}{3}$ yard pink velvet
$2\frac{2}{3}$ yards ecru lace, 1 inch wide
1 yard grosgrain ribbon, $\frac{1}{4}$ inch wide
Polyester fiberfill stuffing
Potpourri (optional)
DMC Mouline embroidery floss

2 skeins #309 deep pink
3 skeins #335 deep pink
3 skeins #899 medium pink
3 skeins #3326 medium pink

3 skeins #776 pale pink
2 skeins #818 pale pink
1 skein #989 green

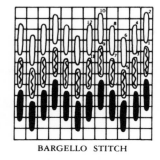

BARGELLO STITCH

SPECIAL HINTS

Draw a line down the center of the canvas and use it as a starting point for each row. For each side, work from this center line to the outer edge. Use a working frame for more refined results.

Finished piece is 8 inches high and 8 inches wide at the widest point.

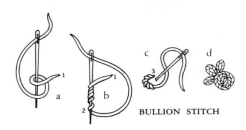

BULLION STITCH

INSTRUCTIONS
background

Cut the embroidery floss into 24-inch lengths. Separate the strands, and add three more strands to each; your working thread will have a total of nine strands. The bargello rhythm is over four threads, with a step of one. The following chart indicates color, row, and number of stitches.

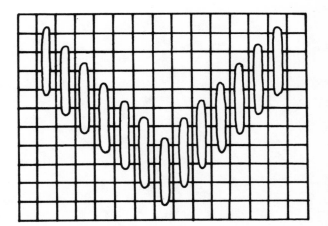

BARGELLO RHYTHM

#309 deep pink	row 1	63 stitches
	row 2	68 stitches
	row 3	73 stitches
#335	row 4	76 stitches
	row 5	79 stitches
	row 6	82 stitches
#899 medium pink	row 7, 8, 9	82 stitches each
#3326	row 10	82 stitches
	row 11	81 stitches
	row 12	80 stitches
#776 pale pink	row 13	79 stitches
	row 14	78 stitches
	row 15	77 stitches
#818 palest pink	row 16	76 stitches
	row 17	77 stitches
	row 18	75 stitches
#776	rows 19–21	2 stitches less each row
#3326	rows 22–24	2 stitches less each row
#899	rows 25–27	2 stitches less each row

115

Make the end of following rows level with row 27 across the top of heart.

#355	rows 28–30
#309	rows 31–33

flower

Use a full six strands of DMC floss and work bullion stitches, curling them around one another to create a cluster of petals. Use #818, and wrap it around your needle nine times for the five center petals. Use #3326, and wrap it thirteen times for the next five petals. Use #989 green, and wrap it twenty-one times for the three leaves. Loop the stitches to create the leaf shape.

FINISHING

Trim the excess canvas $\frac{1}{4}$ inch from the needlework. Stay stitch around the canvas edge and around the needlework edge. Gather the lace to make a ruffle; distribute the gathered edge evenly along the outer edge of the needlework, with the ruffle facing the center of the heart. Pin it in place, and stitch as close to the needlework as possible.

Trace the heart on velvet, and cut it to size. With right sides facing, stitch the pieces together, leaving a 6-inch opening at one side. Turn the heart right side out, and press the seams with your fingers. Stuff well with polyester fiberfill. Add potpourri if desired. Use blind stitches to close. Tie a bow at the center of the ribbon, and sew it at the center top of the heart.

VARIATIONS ON A THEME

The heart pillow can be a memorable ring bearer's pillow. Just add a small piece of ribbon at the center to secure the rings. It can also be a most personal valentine with embroidered names and sentiments. (See graphed alphabets, pages 119 and 165.)

Initials

DEXTERITY: Level I

STITCH
Continental

MATERIALS
Tapestry needle #24
Perforated paper, 2¾ by 5½ inches
Hand-dyed silk twist
    1 skein blue
    1 skein mustard
DMC embroidery floss
    1 skein #356 rust
    1 skein #928 blue-grey
    1 skein #931 blue
1 small piece of batting, 2¼ by 5 inches
1¾ yards mustard velvet ribbon, ¼ inch wide
⅜ yard felt for lining
½ yard print fabric for cover
2 photo mat boards, 11 by 14 inches

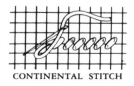

CONTINENTAL STITCH

SPECIAL HINTS

The size of the paper, mat board, and fabric will vary according to the size of the monogram and the desired measurements of the portfolio. Allow a paper margin of 1 inch around the edge of the monogram and a fabric margin of 1 inch around the edge of the mat board.

First choose the fabric for the portfolio; then choose yarns of a light and a dark shade of one color, and a contrasting color, as shown in Color Plate I/J. Perforated paper, comparable to manila tag in weight, is fragile. The proper size for your needle and the thickness of your yarn are important considerations; the needle and yarn must not force the holes to bulge out of shape.

Keep your tension loose so your working thread does not cut through the paper in between your stitches. Hold the paper carefully; do not bend it while you work, as the creases will not always iron out. Be sure to end each section and cut the tail close. Do not skip across the back with your working thread or it will show through the holes.

Yes, it is fragile, but it's so much fun!

The finished piece is 11 inches wide and 14 inches high.

INSTRUCTIONS
letters

Mark the center of your paper by dividing it into equal quarters. Space your letters evenly, making small pencil marks on the back (rough side) of your paper. Ten spaces are the border; letters are five spaces apart and eighteen spaces high, centered within thirty-eight spaces.

Use a single strand of silk twist and continental stitches over one space. Optional highlights of a contrasting yarn were added to the edges of each letter to give them more depth and to make them blend with the border, thus complimenting the fabric.

border

Start at the lower right-hand corner; leave two holes all around the edge as you work, making a five-hole border around the entire monogram.

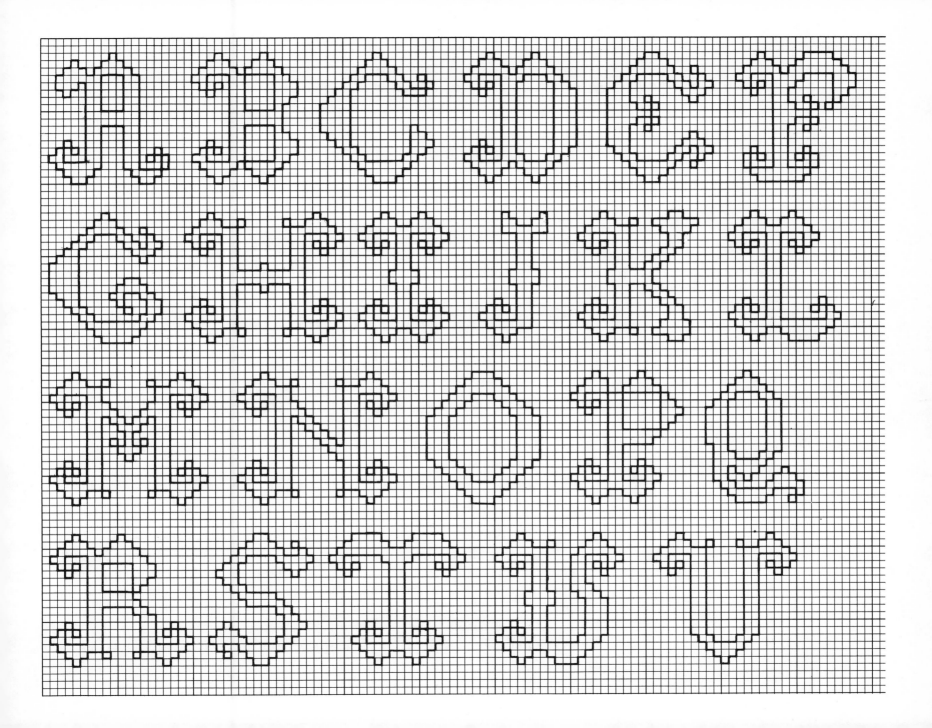

To mark one's personal belongings with initials is a time-honored tradition.

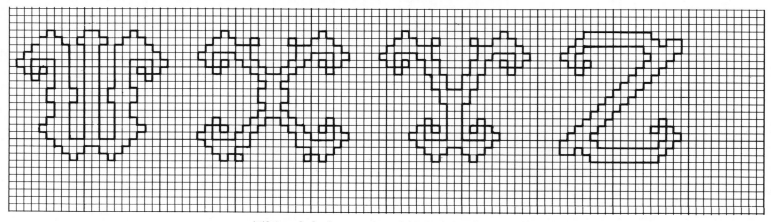

This alphabet was published by Butterick in 1893 in **Artistic Alphabets for Marking and Engrossing.**

Row 1: Use a single strand of floss #356, and work a continental stitch over two spaces.

Row 2: Use a single strand of floss #928, and work a continental stitch over one space.

Row 3: Use a single strand of floss #931, and work a continental stitch over one space.

FINISHING

Cut the fabric, allowing a fabric margin of 1 inch around all the sides and $\frac{1}{2}$ inch at the center fold, when open. Glue the mat board in place. Miter the corners, folding over the fabric margin toward the inside and gluing it in place.

For the batting: Cut the batting $\frac{1}{2}$ inch narrower than the size of your perforated paper. Glue it in place where your monogram will cover it, to give the monogram a fullness and to prevent the printed fabric from showing through the holes.

Glue the monogram to the front, around the border only, so the glue will not show. Glue the narrow ribbon around the edge as a border. For the ties, cut the excess ribbon in half, and glue it in place at the center of the opening.

For the lining: Cut the felt within $\frac{1}{2}$ inch of the edges; glue it in the center fold and all around the edges.

VARIATIONS ON A THEME

This personalized paperwork can be glued onto many surfaces—a diary, guest book, address book, phone book cover, to name a few.

CONTINENTAL STITCH

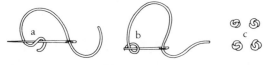

FRENCH KNOT

DEXTERITY: Level I

STITCHES

Continental stitch: letters and leaves
French knots: flowers

MATERIALS

Tapestry needle #24
Perforated paper, 6 by 8 inches
Oval frame, 8 by 10 inches
Hand-dyed silk twist or DMC Perle cotton, #3 weight
1 skein #550 purple
1 skein #472 chartreuse
DMC Mouline embroidery floss
1 skein #828 light blue

SPECIAL HINTS

Handle the paper carefully to avoid tearing it. Trace the oval-frame opening on the back of the paper. Determine the midpoint, counting holes

from top to bottom and side to side. Determine the starting point by counting up sixteen holes from the midpoint, and over two holes to the right.

Finished piece is 10 inches wide and 8 inches high.

INSTRUCTIONS

letters

Use a single strand of silk twist or Perle cotton #3 in purple. Begin working the continental stitch at the starting point, with the top left-side letter O. Complete the letter O, then work J and Y in proper position on either side, spaced evenly within the frame. Follow the graph.

leaves

Use a single strand of silk twist or Perle cotton #3 in chartreuse and work a continental stitch. Follow the graph.

flowers

Use a full six strands of DMC Mouline embroidery floss in light blue, and make French knots according to the graph.

FINISHING

Trim the excess paper to fit the needlework into the frame. Glue the paper directly to the wooden frame on the back, all around the recessed molding.

VARIATIONS ON A THEME

Joy is one of many exclamations you may choose to work. You can use the finished piece as a personal greeting or valentine, or without the frame as a book mark.

King

DEXTERITY: Level III

MATERIALS

Stretcher frame, 24 by 36 inches
1 yard of jungle-print fabric
Disposable canvas, 9 by 12 inches
Tapestry needle #22
Paternayan Persian 3-ply wool
DMC Mouline embroidery floss
DMC Perle cotton, #3 weight
Mohair Knitting wool
Poster board or felt for backing, cut to fit frame

		PERSIAN YARN	
DESIGN AREA	**STITCHES**	*Amount*	*Color*
Face	Continental stitch	15 strands	#496 light beige
		20 strands	#492 medium beige
		10 strands	#462 dark beige
Chin	Encroaching Gobelin stitch	*	#496 light beige

CONTINENTAL STITCH

ENCROACHING GOBELIN

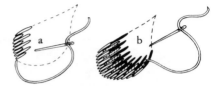

LONG AND SHORT STITCHES

			MOHAIR KNITTING YARN	
	Long and short stitches	1 skein	beige-gold	
Mane	Long and short stitches	*	beige-gold	
			EMBROIDERY FLOSS	
Nose	Continental stitch	1 skein	#938 brown	
			PERLE COTTON	
Eyes	Continental stitch	1 skein	#975 brown	
		1 skein	#977 gold	
		1 skein	#938 brown	
Whiskers	Straight stitch	1 skein	#712 white	

* Use remainder of yarn from other design areas.

SPECIAL HINTS

Wrap the fabric around the stretcher frame, and staple it at the back. Baste the disposable canvas to the front of the fabric. Fold the yarn in half and place the ends together. Work without a tail so there is less bulk through the fabric.

Finished piece is 24 inches wide and 36 inches high.

INSTRUCTIONS

face

Use two strands of a 3-ply Persian yarn, and work a continental stitch simultaneously through the canvas and the fabric. Follow the graph for a color guide.

nose

Use four strands of 6-ply embroidery floss, work continental stitches, and follow the graph. Use two strands folded in half for your working thread.

eyes

Use two strands of Perle cotton, #975 brown and #977 gold, and four strands of floss, #938 brown. Work in continental stitches, following the graph.

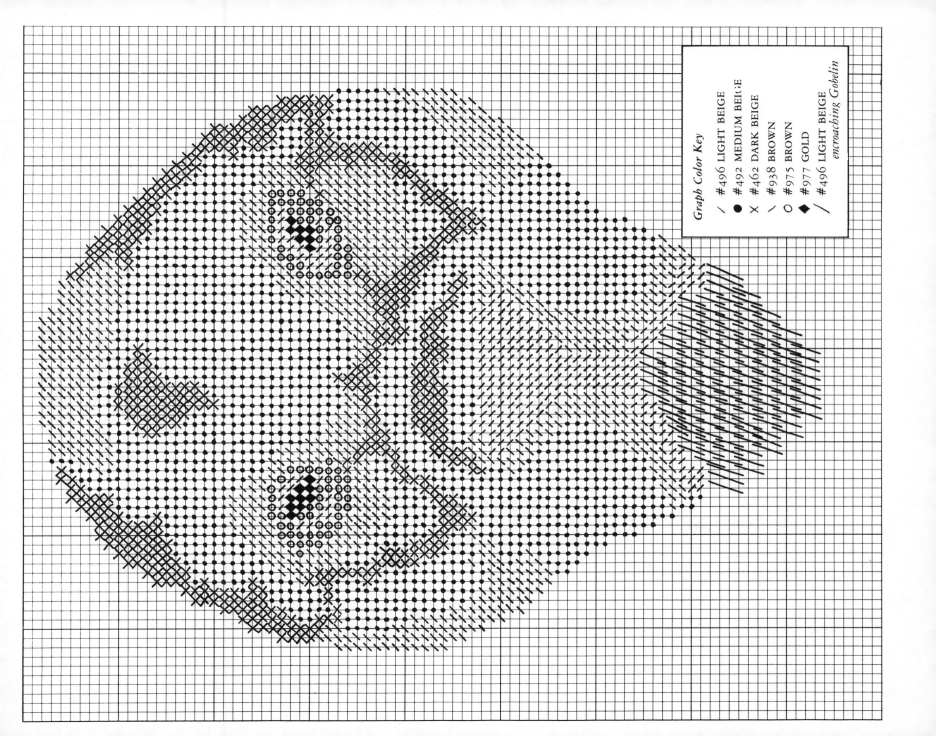

Graph Color Key

/ #496 LIGHT BEIGE
● #492 MEDIUM BEIGE
X #462 DARK BEIGE
\ #938 BROWN
○ #975 BROWN
◆ #977 GOLD
/ #496 LIGHT BEIGE
encroaching Gobelin

chin

Use two strands of #496 light beige, and work an encroaching Gobelin stitch over four threads, following the graph. Highlight with random long and short stitches of multicolor mohair yarn.

mane

Use a single strand of multicolor mohair, and make long and short stitches. Start at the chin with the short stitches, making them 1 inch long, and taper to $\frac{1}{2}$ inch long at the corner of the nose. Continue around the head; start with 1$\frac{1}{2}$-inch stitches and gradually enlarge to 3- and 4-inch stitches at the top of the mane. Vary the length of the stitches for a hairy effect. Work the other half in the same manner. Cut a few stitches at random, for shagginess.

whiskers

Use a single strand of white Perle cotton, and work six or eight straight stitches in a random pattern to make whiskers. Spray with hair spray to avoid their drooping.

FINISHING

Dampen the disposable canvas with a wet sponge, making it easier to remove, and remove it by pulling out the threads individually, through the yarn. Since the fabric is wrapped around a stretcher frame, the needlework is self-framed. Cover the raw back with poster board or felt.

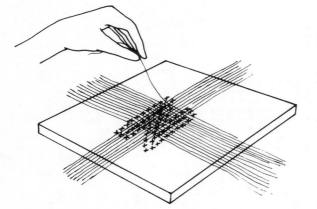

Removing disposable canvas threads

Love

DEXTERITY: Level II

STITCHES

    Rococo stitch: heart
    Continental stitch: letters
    Brick stitch: background
    Straight stitch: highlights

MATERIALS

    Tapestry needle #20
    Mono canvas #14, $\frac{1}{3}$ yard
    French wool
        1 hank (4 skeins, 100 strands each) #502 ecru
    French silk
        2 skeins (10 yards each) #2924 red
        1 skein (10 yards) #2914 rose
        1 skein (10 yards) #2912 pink
    Copper embroidery thread, 4 yards
    Picture frame, 8 by 10 inches
    Plywood or photo mat board cut to size
    Butterfly pin or button (optional)

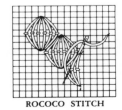

ROCOCO STITCH

CONTINENTAL STITCH

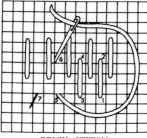

BRICK STITCH

SPECIAL HINTS

It is advisable to use a working frame for uniform results since the pulled work requires a taut canvas.

Finished piece is 15 inches wide and 13½ inches high.

INSTRUCTIONS

letters

Use a single strand of French silk in the color indicated, a full 7-ply, and work a continental stitch from bottom to top, according to the graph. First do letter *L*, then *V* and *E*.

heart

Use a single strand of 7-ply French silk in the color indicated, separated for fullness, and make a rococo stitch, starting at the bottom—eighteen threads from the *L*. Work the following rows:

Row 1: Work one stitch.

Row 2: Work two stitches.

Row 3: Work three stitches.

Row 4: Work four stitches.

Row 5: Work four stitches, and finish the row with one compensating stitch worked around the *V*.

Row 6: Work four stitches and one compensating stitch; end with one full stitch.

Row 7: Work four stitches, one compensating stitch, and two more stitches.

Row 8: Work four stitches, skip under the *V,* and work three more stitches.

Row 9: Work the right half of a rococo stitch, three full stitches; skip under the *V*, and work two full stitches, ending with the left half of a rococo stitch.

Row 10: Work four stitches, the bottom half of a rococo stitch, and one full stitch; repeat the bottom half of a rococo stitch, and end with three full stitches.

Graph Color Key

✕ #2914 ROSE

● #2912 PINK

　#2924 RED—*heart*

❘ COPPER

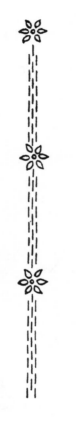

Row 11: Work three stitches on either side of the heart, skipping one full stitch in the center.

Row 12: Work two stitches on either side of the heart, skipping three full stitches in the center. Fill in top spaces with the bottom half of a rococo stitch in between the two full stitches you have just worked, to create a heart shape.

background

Use six strands of French wool and work a brick stitch over four threads, with a step of two. Use a half stitch where necessary, to conform to the design. Start in the upper left corner, ten rows above the *L*, and work back and forth to six rows below the *L*.

highlights

Use two strands of copper thread, and make straight stitches to outline and highlight the letters. Suggested areas are on the graph. However, you may wish to use more or less copper according to your personal tastes and the style of your frame.

FINISHING

Remove the needlework from the working frame. Block it, face side up, and attach the butterfly. Mount the piece on plywood or a photo mat board, cut to the proper size, and attach it to the frame.

VARIATIONS ON A THEME

Love can become a pillow or a scrap book cover for someone very special. Be sure to check the dimensions of the surface you need to cover; add to or subtract from the background space to fit the desired project.

Mirror

DEXTERITY: Level I

STITCH

Continental

MATERIALS

Tapestry needle #18

Columbia-Minerva plastic mesh #8060, 10½ by 13½ inches

Boiltex rayon seam binding, ½ inch wide:

6 packages #256 off white

6 packages #10 Monaco blue

4 packages #136C devil red

Mirror, cut to inside frame measurements, 8 by 9¾ inches

Narrow antique-silver inside frame, 8 by 9¾ inches

Wider antique-silver outside frame, 11½ by 14½ inches

SPECIAL HINTS

This is an excellent introductory needlework piece for children; however, you may wish to replace the seam binding with heavy yarn. Plastic mesh can be cut to any size and does not require binding.

Finished piece is 14½ inches wide and 11½ inches high.

CONTINENTAL STITCH

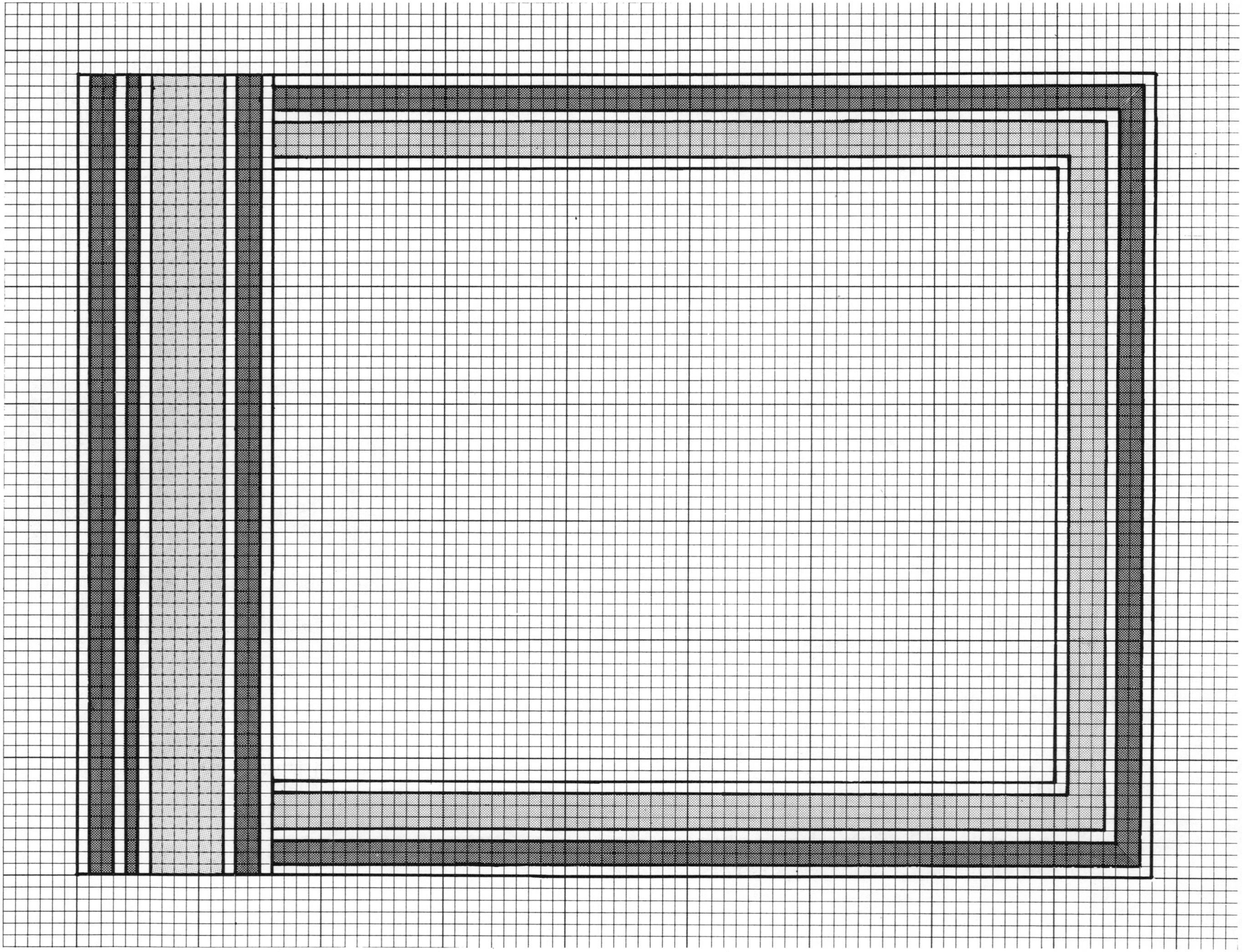

INSTRUCTIONS

Cut the seam binding into thirds, and fold in it half lengthwise ($\frac{1}{4}$ inch wide); press it with a steam iron. Thread the seam binding through the needle, and work in a continental stitch. To start, cover the tail as you work the first few stitches. To stop, run the tail end through the back of the last few stitches; trim excess. Begin work at the left side with the wide stripe; follow the color graph. Continue work at the bottom, right, and top. It is not necessary to stop at the end of these rows. Continue working around; be sure the stitches are at the proper angle.

FINISHING

Cut out the unworked canvas center for the mirror insert. You can bring the canvas to your local frame shop for finishing. Or you may prefer to purchase a framed mirror, insert it inside the needlework, and frame the outside with a ready-made frame. Or, you can leave the entire needlework piece unframed, finish the edges with an additional row of stitches, and glue the needlework mat over a preframed mirror.

VARIATIONS ON A THEME

The mirror can be made into a picture or bulletin board frame. Worked in a stripe or plaid, it could make striking, washable placemats.

Graph Color Key

#10 MONACO BLUE
#256 OFF WHITE
#136C DEVIL RED

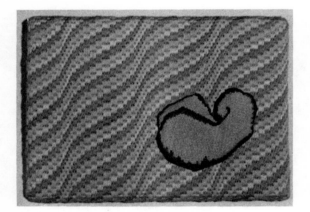

DEXTERITY: Level II

STITCHES
Bargello stitch: background
Continental stitch: seashell

MATERIALS
Tapestry needle #20
Mono canvas #14, 10 by 12 inches
Mono canvas #18, 6 by 6 inches
DMC Mouline cotton embroidery floss ⎫
  2 skeins ecru   ⎬ Seashell
  1 skein #436 gold
  1 skein #801 brown   ⎭

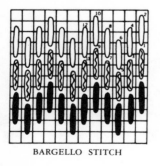

BARGELLO STITCH

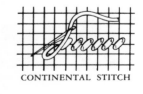

CONTINENTAL STITCH

Lily crochet cotton
    1 skein #4 ecru
DMC embroidery floss
    5 skeins ecru
Paternayan 3-ply Persian } Background
    6 strands #020 ivory
    6 strands #153 pink
    6 strands #015 yellow
Small portion of cotton stuffing
Plywood, $\frac{1}{4}$ inch thick, 6 by 9 inches
Felt square, 6 by 9 inches

SPECIAL HINTS

There are three possible appliqué techniques. Choose the one that suits you best.

• Work the background, and then the seashell. Trim the raw edges of the shell to within $\frac{1}{4}$ inch of the needlework; turn the raw edges under. Stuff the shell with a small portion of cotton as you secure it into place with blind stitches.

• Work the seashell before working the background. Unravel all extra threads from around the needlework. Stuff the shell with cotton as you weave single threads of the shell into the background canvas threads to hold the shell in place. Then work the background over these threads to cover them.

• Work the background first, then the seashell. Stuff and appliqué by unraveling as in method 2, but pull the canvas threads of the shell through to the back of the background canvas with a large-eyed needle, and secure in place with firm knots.

Mark the background area, 7 by 10 inches, on #14 mono canvas; staple it to the working frame. There is no need to attach the smaller canvas to a working frame.

Finished piece is 9 inches wide and 6 inches high.

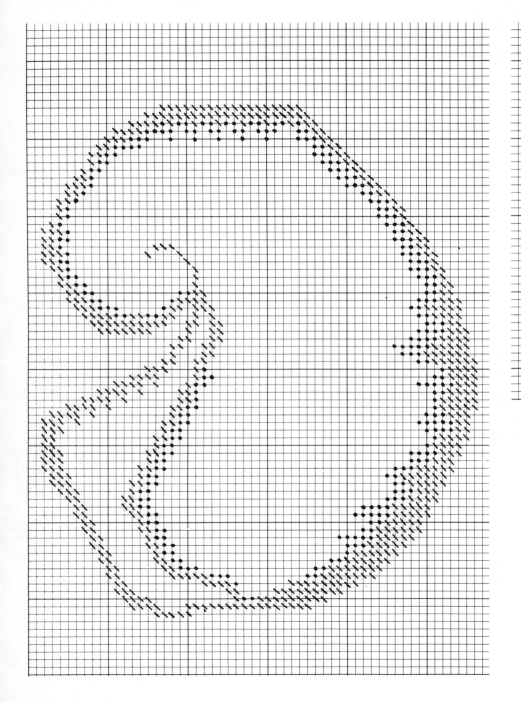

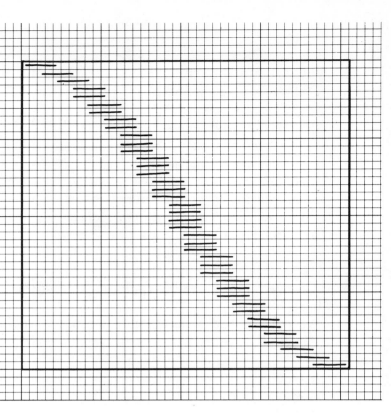

Graph Color Key

● #436 GOLD

╱ #801 BROWN

ECRU—*remainder of shell*

Note: Be sure to include the three single stitches at each end of the bargello unit.

BARGELLO RHYTHM— BACKGROUND

INSTRUCTIONS
seashell

Use a full six strands DMC floss and work a continental stitch; follow the color graph.

background

Start at the lower right corner; use a bargello stitch in the rhythm shown on the graph. For the DMC row, cut the floss into working lengths, separate the strands, and use nine strands as the working thread. For the crochet cotton row, use a doubled strand; thread a single strand through the needle and double over for less bulk (be sure the stitches lie flat).

For the Persian-wool row, use two single strands in the following order: in the first wool row, one pink and one yellow; in the second wool row, one yellow and one ivory; in the third wool row, one pink and one ivory. Repeat this order of color throughout the background.

FINISHING

Remove the completed appliqué canvas from the working frame. Cut a piece of 6- by 9-inch plywood; wrap the needlework around the plywood, and staple it to the back. Cut the felt to cover the raw back, and glue it in place. Nail a picture hanger to the center back of the plywood.

VARIATIONS ON A THEME

Nautilus would make a smashing cover for a ship's log.

Ocean

DEXTERITY: Level III

STITCHES

    Bargello stitch: waves
    French knots: foam

MATERIALS

    Tapestry needle #20
    Mono canvas #16, 14 inches square
    Yarn—light to dark shades
        1 skein Bella Donna #845 silver, 1 working strand
        1 skein DMC Mouline #762 silver, 9 working strands
        1 skein DMC Mouline #415 grey, 9 working strands
        1 skein DMC Mouline #775 blue, 9 working strands
        1 skein DMC Mouline #747 aqua, 9 working strands
        2 skeins Fawcett linen 20/2 aqua, 2 working strands
        2 skeins DMC Mouline #928 sage, 9 working strands
        1 skein DMC Mouline #927 green, 9 working strands
        2 skeins Perle cotton, #3 weight #932 blue, 1 working strand
        1 skein DMC Mouline #931 sage, 9 working strands

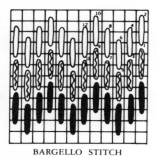

BARGELLO STITCH

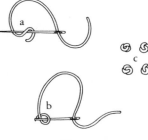

FRENCH KNOT

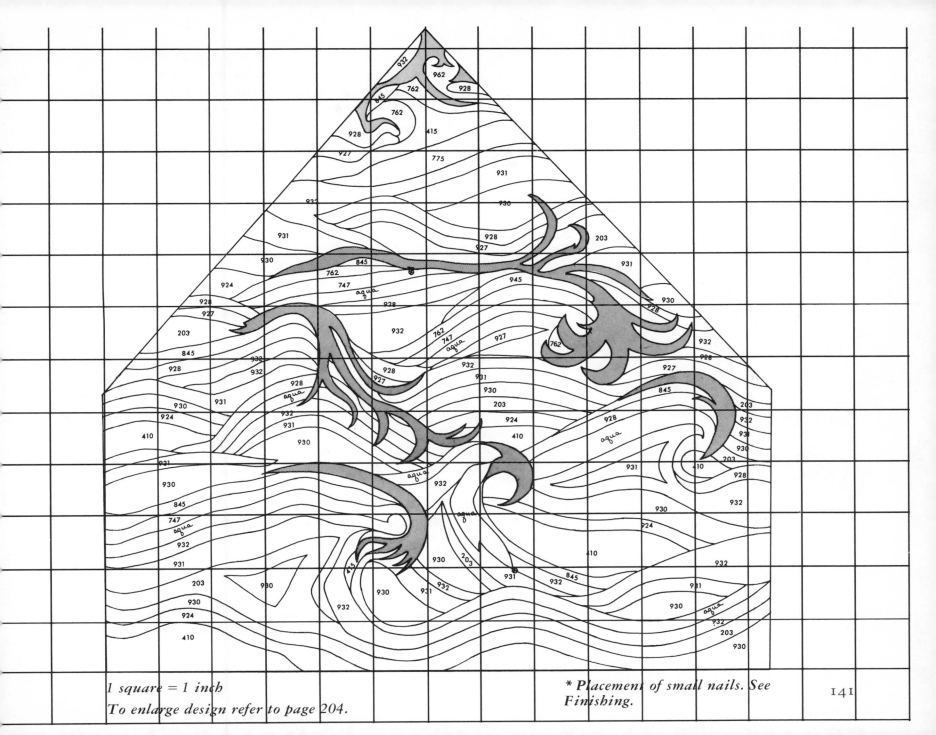

1 square = 1 inch

To enlarge design refer to page 204.

* Placement of small nails. See
Finishing.

141

1 skein Medici wool #203 sage, 4 working strands
2 skeins Perle cotton, #3 weight #930 sage, 1 working strand
1 skein DMC Mouline #924 sage, 9 working strands
1 skein Medici wool #410 sage, 4 working strands
Plywood, ¼ inch thick and 12 inches square
2 smoky-glass mirrors, 9 inches square
3 angle brackets and a few nails with very small heads
Small amount of polyester fiberfill

SPECIAL HINTS

It is advisable to use a working frame. Staple the canvas in place. Use the number of strands suggested in the materials list for your working thread. Finished piece is 11½ inches wide, 12 inches deep, and 9 inches high.

INSTRUCTIONS

waves

Draw the outline of each wave onto the canvas. Work from the top of each wave to the bottom—so any compensating stitches are not as visible. Work the bargello-stitch waves over four threads, with a step of one. Work the bargello stitch first, then embellish with French knots for the foam effect. Use the illustration as a guide to shape and shades. Not all colors are used in every wave. Precise copying of stitches is not mandatory for a final effect; use your discretion.

foam

Use a single strand of Bella Donna rayon #845 silver, and work a French knot stitch. Mass several knots together for a three-dimensional foam effect.

FINISHING

Remove the canvas from the working frame. Cut the plywood to the specified shape. Wrap the needlework around the plywood, overlapping the bottom and the two short straight sides. Staple the piece in place, but leave one top side open. Stuff with a small amount of polyester fiberfill in one front corner, one center corner, and the top. Finish stapling the needlework to the plywood. Nail down the canvas with small nails in two or three places to create the illusion of ocean swells.

Cut the mirrors to the specified shape. Place the short edges together at the peak of the needlework triangle. Hold them in place with angle brackets, and screw them into the bottom of the plywood.

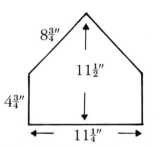

Cut the plywood to the correct shape

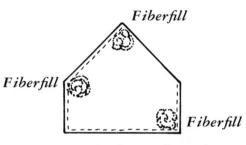

Staple the needlework part-way around and stuff with fiberfill

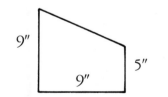

Cut the mirrors to the correct shape

Pillow

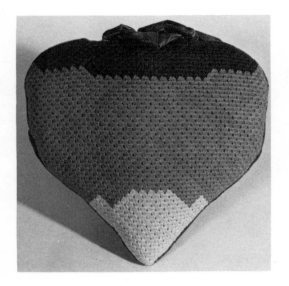

ROCOCO STITCH

DEXTERITY: Level II

STITCH

    Rococo stitch: berry

MATERIALS

    Tapestry needle #22
    Mono canvas #18, 12 inches square
    DMC Mouline embroidery floss
        4 skeins #894 pale pink
       17 skeins #892 deep pink
        6 skeins #816 deep red
    White fabric for lining, 12 inches square
    Berry-color fabric for backing, 12 inches square
    Polyester fiberfill for stuffing, 1 small package
    $\frac{2}{3}$ yard green ribbon, $1\frac{1}{2}$ inches wide, for leaves

SPECIAL HINTS

    Staple the canvas to a working frame. Start working at the bottom and work toward the top, since each stitch builds upon the next stitch. Work in a

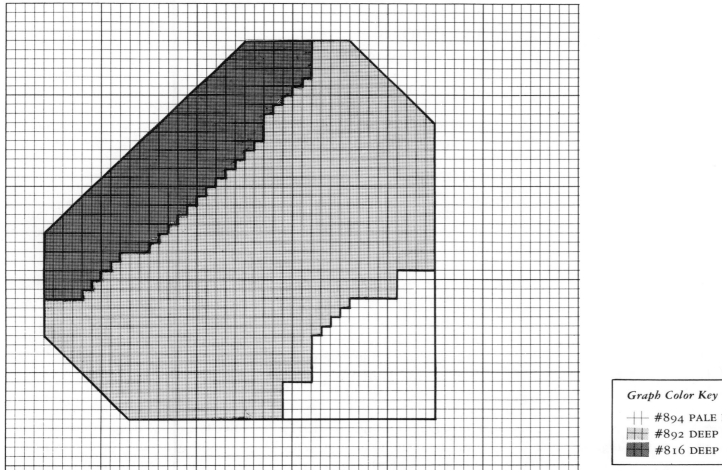

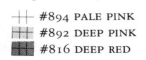

Graph Color Key

╫ #894 PALE PINK
▦ #892 DEEP PINK
▓ #816 DEEP RED

Each diamond equals one rococo stitch

diagonal direction so your yarn will not cover any holes as you move onto the next stitch. Complete one color before you change to the next section, for ease in following the graph.

Finished piece is 10 inches high and 10 inches wide at the widest point.

INSTRUCTIONS
berry

Use a full six strands of DMC floss and work a rococo stitch. As you work, enlarge the holes for the top and bottom of each rococo stitch. A large hole is necessary so the lining fabric can show through as seeds. Follow the graph; fill in with a half stitch where necessary to conform to the shape of the design—that is, across the top and sides.

FINISHING
lining

Cut the canvas from the frame to within $\frac{1}{4}$ inch of the needlework. Stitch the white fabric to the back of the canvas around the entire edge; sew as close to the needlework as possible. Trim excess fabric.

backing

Use the berry as a pattern to cut the backing fabric. With right sides together, sew the backing fabric to the berry front, leaving 4 inches open at the top center for stuffing. Trim excess fabric. Turn right sides out, and press the seams flat with your fingers. Stuff with polyester fiberfill until plump.

leaves

Cut the ribbon into two strips 3 inches long, and three strips 5 inches long. Fold the two small strips and the one large strip in half to form a triangle. With the large strip in the center, folded sides up, sew the edges of the ribbon to the raw edge of the berry opening. Make two loops from the other two long strips; sew the raw edges of the ribbon to the other side of the berry opening.

FRONT   BACK

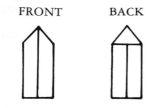

Fold to form a triangle

ENLARGED VIEW

berry

Be sure the berry is plump enough at the top opening; add more stuffing if necessary. Make blind stitches to close, using matching thread.

VARIATIONS ON A THEME

The strawberry pillow can be made into a bun warmer. Instead of stuffing it, line it with a quilted cotton fabric and add a zipper at the opening. With the same technique and the addition of a green cord shoulder strap, the pillow can be made into a purse.

Quilt

DEXTERITY: Level III

This needlework piece is not for the novice. Long dedicated hours go into the making of so many patches. I consider the piece an heirloom; this thought makes one's work pleasurable and gives it a most satisfying purpose.

Each patch in the quilt is meaningful to our family, commemorating favorite places, important events, personal memories. My children each designed their own patches, and we hope that future generations will add theirs. Perhaps this humble beginning will one day become something quite splendiferous! A favorite quotation from an old sampler was the inspiration for it all: "To my children I bequeath these things. One is roots, the other wings."

The real joy of the quilt is that it is a *personal* chronicle which immortalizes the personalities, characteristics, quirks, and charms of your family. To start, list the specific ideas you might want to interpret into patches, then work out each design on graph paper. Be sure to consider the scale of each design and the stitches it will require before you start to work the patch.

To help you begin, there is a pattern outline of the thirty-four patches in the quilt. Some special patches are graphed and explained in detail for you to follow or be inspired by, as you prefer. If you create all new patches, the patch shapes may change from the pattern outline given here; in that case, just use this outline as a starting point.

The other projects in the book have designs, stitches, and techniques that can be the inspiration for your patches. You can adapt the evergreens from Album, the strawberry from Pillow, the pansy from Flowers, the rainbow from Rainbow, and the scallop from Shell.

Many of the stitches form lovely patterns in themselves. The leaf stitch, double straight cross-stitch, diamond eyelet, and wheat stitch each would work beautifully filling in a patch. You can also use the tent stitch as a background and then work embroidery—lazy daisy, French knots—over it. Long satin stitches also work well with embroidery over them. The bargello patterns from other projects in the book can also be used; or use your own favorites. And do consider the beautiful yarns and flosses used in the projects for special textures and effects in your patches.

Some of the inspirations for my patches may help to inspire yours: favorite flowers, your pets (their paw prints can find their way into a patch), places you've visited (evergreens, sand dunes, tile roofs, wheat fields, brick roads), your favorite things (stars, books, a teddy bear, shamrocks, rainbows, snowflakes), signs of the zodiac, your signature, your personal symbol. You'll find that most everything that symbolizes you and your family can be interpreted into a patch design. If you wish, a favorite quotation can be embroidered into the ribbon border.

MATERIALS

The yarn requirements for the patches given in detail are listed separately. The materials required in addition to the yarns are as follows:

Tapestry needle #22

Mono canvas #18, cut 18 inches by 18 inches

Working frame, 18 inches square

$2\frac{1}{2}$ yards moiré ribbon ($1\frac{1}{2}$ inches wide)

$\frac{1}{2}$ yard muslin or other backing fabric

3 small curtain loops (for hanging)

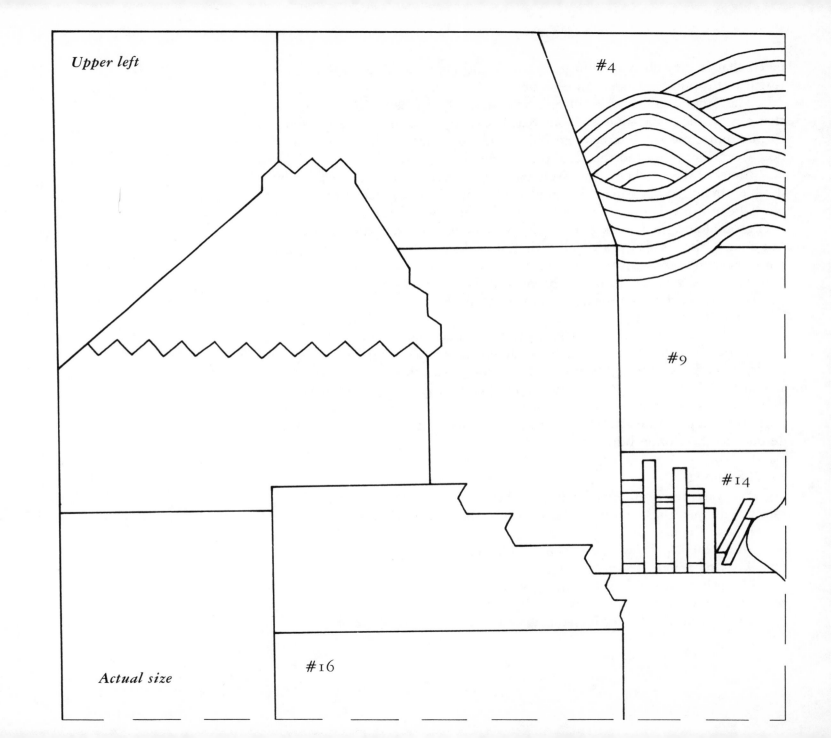

Upper left

#4

#9

#14

Actual size

#16

150

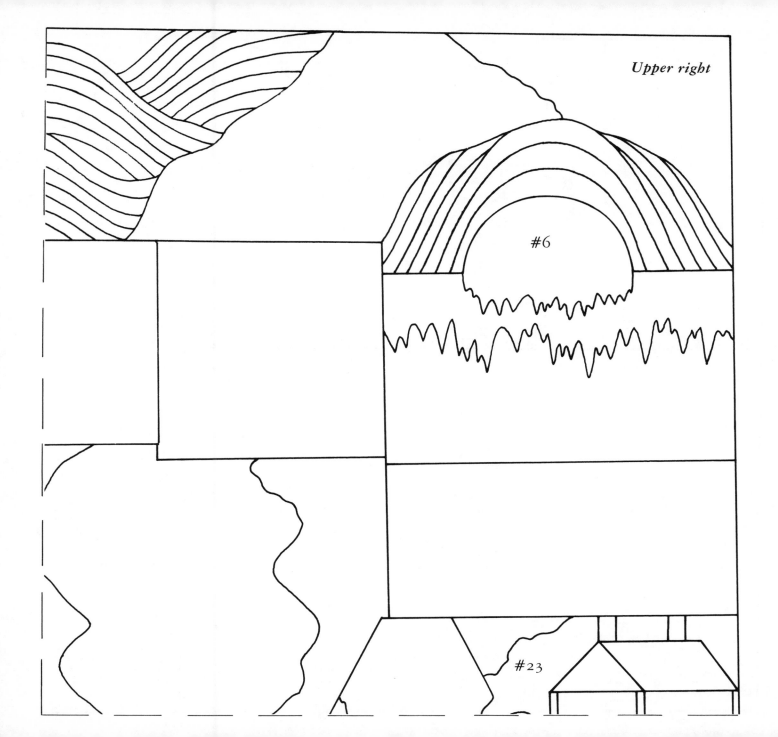

Upper right

#6

#23

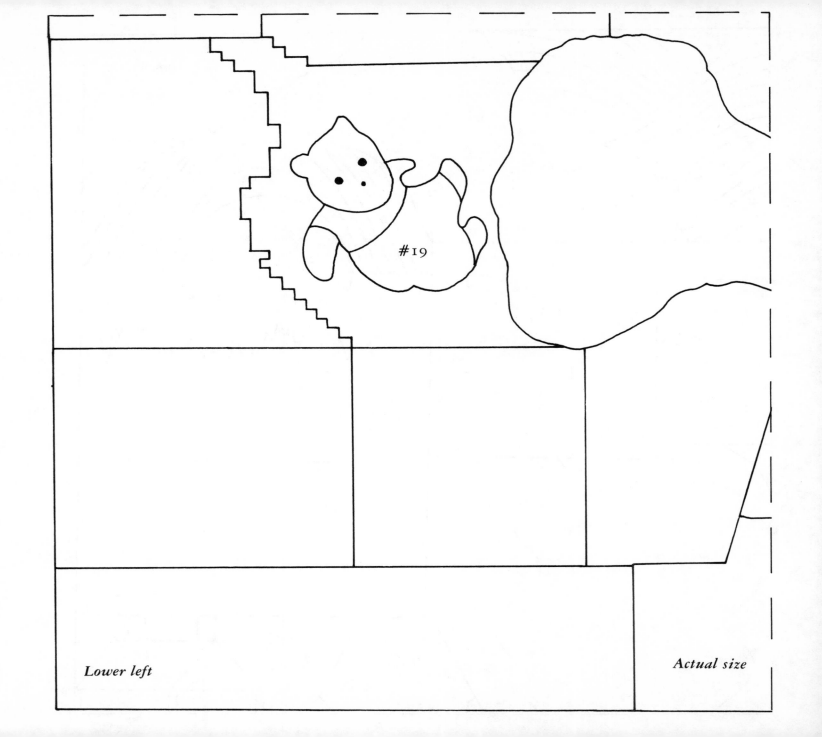

#19

Lower left

Actual size

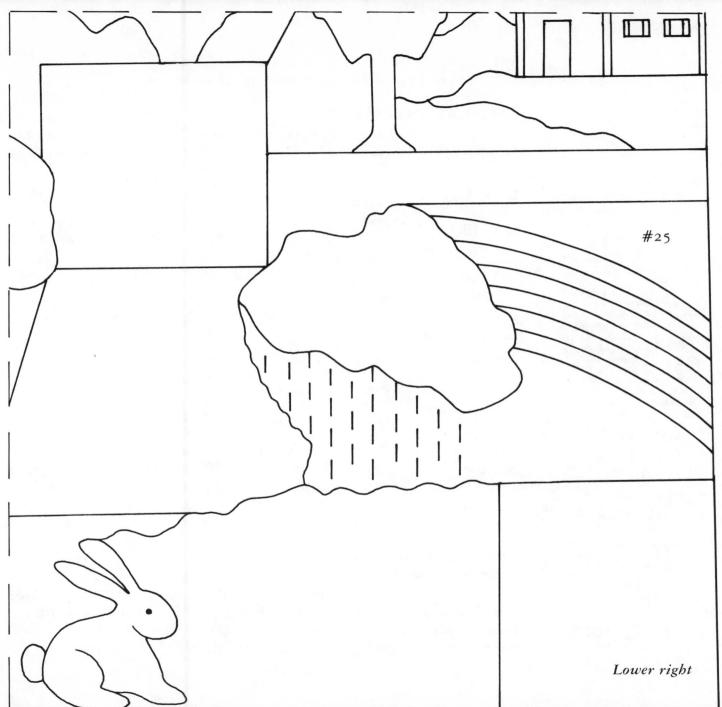

#25

Lower right

SPECIAL HINTS

Finished piece is 18 inches wide and 18 inches high.

GENERAL INSTRUCTIONS

Trace the pattern outline (given here in four parts) onto tissue paper and then onto your canvas with a hard lead pencil. Staple the canvas to a working frame.

Patch #4: Dunes

MATERIALS

DMC embroidery floss
Hand-dyed silk twist

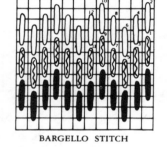

BARGELLO STITCH

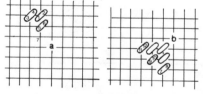

BASKETWEAVE STITCH

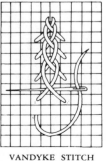

VANDYKE STITCH

DESIGN AREA	STITCHES	EMBROIDERY FLOSS	
		Amount	*Color*
Dunes	Bargello stitch	16 yards	ecru
		9 yards	# 644 sand
		SILK TWIST	
		7 yards	white
		EMBROIDERY FLOSS	
Beach	Basketweave stitch	16 yards	ecru
Sea grass	Straight stitch	1 yard	#3055 sea green
Dusty Miller (plants)	Vandyke stitch	2 yards	# 938 sage

INSTRUCTIONS

dunes and beach

Start the dune at the top and work the bargello stitches over three threads in a random rhythm to conform to the outlines. For the first row use nine strands of DMC ecru. Follow with DMC sand, then the white silk. Repeat the sequence of yarns as you work. Work each successive row in the same random rhythm until each dune is complete. Use a full strand of ecru floss and work basketweave stitches to fill in the beach.

sea grass
With two separated strands of green DMC floss, work a few small, but loose, straight stitches to resemble clumps of sea grass.

dusty miller
Use a full strand of sage floss and work a group of Vandyke stitches close together to resemble dusty miller.

Patch #6: Sunset

MATERIALS
Marlitt
DMC embroidery floss
Hand-dyed silk twist

DESIGN AREA	STITCHES	Amount	Color
		MARLITT	
Sun	Satin stitch	6 yards	#1003 umber
		EMBROIDERY FLOSS	
Sky	Bargello stitch	2 yards	# 436 dark gold
		2 yards	# 437 gold
		5 yards	# 738 dark yellow
		4 yards	# 739 yellow
		SILK TWIST	
Reflection	Encroaching oblique stitch	3 yards	peach
		4 yards	plum
		3 yards	lavender
		4 yards	light blue
		4 yards	blue

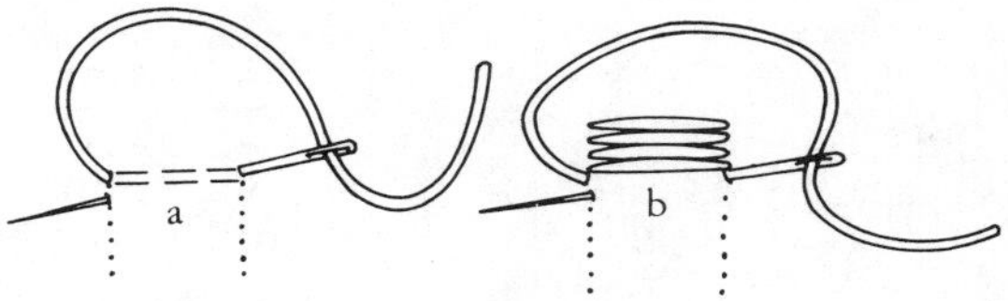

SATIN STITCH

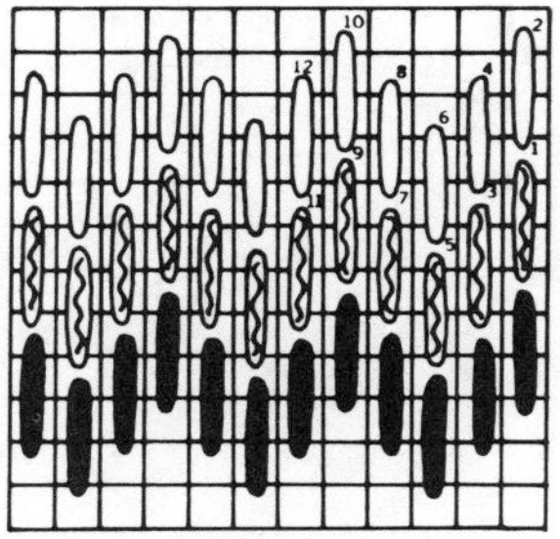

BARGELLO STITCH

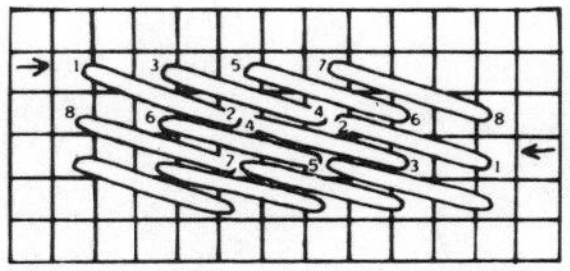

ENCROACHING OBLIQUE STITCH

INSTRUCTIONS

With a double strand of Marlitt, work the sun in a satin stitch. Form an archway at the top of the sun and create a jagged edge at the bottom to give the illusion of the sun sinking below the horizon. Work the sky with nine strands of DMC floss and bargello stitches. Start with deep gold and work outward to yellow. For the reflection, use a single strand of silk twist and work an encroaching oblique stitch over four threads. Working in a vertical direction, use the peach shade first, then plum, followed by lavender, pale blue, and blue. Work in a random pattern to create a striated reflection of the sun.

Patch #9: Quilt

MATERIALS
DMC embroidery floss
Hand-dyed silk twist

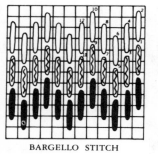

BARGELLO STITCH

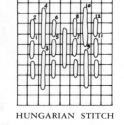

HUNGARIAN STITCH

DESIGN AREA	STITCHES	EMBROIDERY FLOSS	
		Amount	*Color*
Patchwork design	Bargello stitch	1 yard	# 758 pale brick
		1 yard	# 316 lavender
		2 yards	# 315 plum
		1 yard	#3053 green
		SILK TWIST	
Background	Hungarian stitch	6 yards	pale brick
Patchwork outline	Straight stitch	*	pale brick

* Use remainder of yarn from other design areas

INSTRUCTIONS

With a full six strands of DMC floss, work the patchwork pattern in a bargello stitch over three threads, according to the color graph. Then work the background with a single strand of silk twist in a Hungarian stitch done

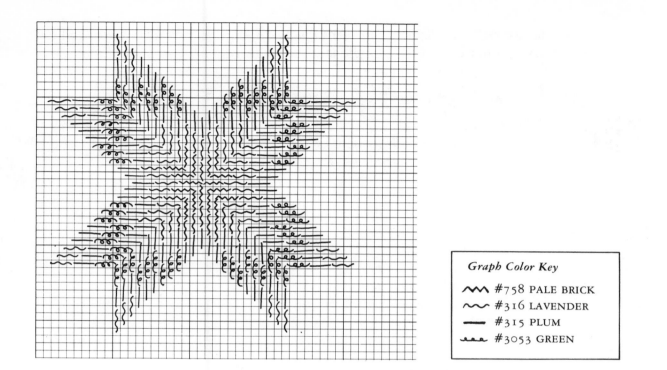

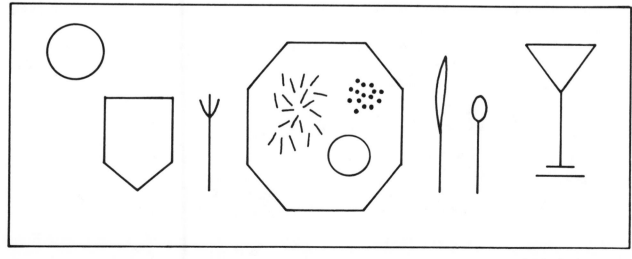

Actual size

horizontally. Upon completion of the patch, outline the quilt pattern and the entire quilt edge with a single strand of silk twist in a straight stitch.

Patch #14: Books

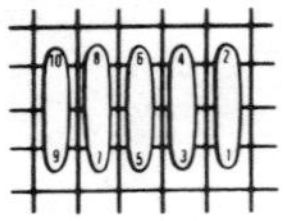

STITCHES

Horizontal Gobelin stitch: books
Basketweave stitch: background

MATERIALS

DMC embroidery floss
2 yards #935 green
1 yard #632 brown
3 yards #815 red
2 yards #642 taupe
4 yards #3371 dark brown
1 yard gold metallic embroidery thread

INSTRUCTIONS

Work the books with a double strand of DMC floss in a horizontal Gobelin stitch. Work from left to right: one green book spine over four threads; one brown book spine over two threads; one red book spine over three threads; one taupe book spine over three threads; one red book spine over three threads; one green book spine over two threads. Work the background in a basketweave stitch.

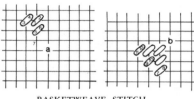

GOBELIN
STITCH

BASKETWEAVE STITCH

Patch #16: Table Setting

MATERIALS

DMC embroidery floss	Linen yarn
Embroidery thread	Perle cotton, #3 weight
Hand-dyed silk twist	14 silver glass beads

DESIGN AREA	STITCHES	Amount	Color
		EMBROIDERY FLOSS	
Plate	Basketweave stitch	3 yards	# 739 cream
Plate outline	Straight stitch	1 yard	# 832 blue
Background	Basketweave stitch	10 yards	# 738 pale gold
Wine	Satin stitch	½ yard	# 902 wine
Peas	French knots	1 yard	#3012 green
Carrots	Straight stitch	1 yard	# 922 orange
Lettuce	Loop stitch	1 yard	#3013 pale green
		EMBROIDERY THREAD	
Silverware	Straight stitch	1 yard	silver
		SILK TWIST	
Napkin	Satin stitch	1 yard	white
		LINEN YARN	
Salad bowl	Raised cup stitch	1 yard	russet
		BEADS	
Wine glass	Sewing stitch	14 beads	silver
		PERLE COTTON	
Hamburger	Raised cup stitch	½ yard	# 938 dark brown

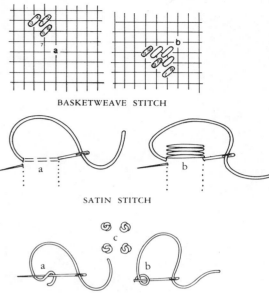

BASKETWEAVE STITCH

SATIN STITCH

FRENCH KNOT

LOOP STITCH

INSTRUCTIONS

Work the plate with a full strand of floss in a basketweave stitch. Then work the entire background. Outline the plate with a single strand of blue floss in a straight stitch. Place the silverware in the proper position with a double strand of silver embroidery thread. Use a double strand of white silk twist and work satin stitches for the damask napkin. Use a double strand of russet linen and work a raised cup stitch to create a salad bowl. With a beading needle and sewing thread, stitch the glass beads in place to form a crystal wine glass. Fill the glass with wine by working a satin stitch with a full strand of wine floss. The peas are made with a full strand of pea green floss and a group of French knots. The carrots are made with a full strand of orange floss and small straight stitches placed at random. The hamburger is

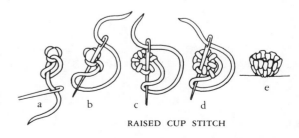

RAISED CUP STITCH

made with a single strand of dark brown Perle cotton in a raised cup stitch, pulled tightly to form the hamburger. Add lettuce to the salad bowl with a series of small loop stitches worked in pale green floss.

Patch #19: Bear

MATERIALS
DMC embroidery floss
Hand-dyed silk twist

DESIGN AREA	STITCHES	EMBROIDERY FLOSS	
		Amount	*Color*
Bear's sweater	Continental stitch	1 yard	#815 red
Hands and toes	Continental stitch	*	#676 gold
Bear's body	Turkey work stitch	8 yards	#676 gold
Nose	French knots	*	#815 red
		SILK TWIST	
Eyes	French knots	*	brown
Background	Mosiac stitch	7 yards	brown
		7 yards	dark brown

* Use remainder of yarn from other design areas.

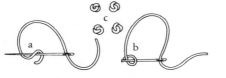

FRENCH KNOT

MOSAIC STITCH

INSTRUCTIONS
With a full strand of red floss, use a continental stitch to work the bear's sweater. With a full strand of gold floss, use a continental stitch to work the bear's toes and hand. With a full strand of gold floss, use a turkey work stitch to work the remainder of the bear. Work the entire bear prior to cutting your stitches or they will tangle. Add a red French knot nose and brown French knot eyes. Fill in the entire background with a mosaic stitch worked

with a single strand of brown and a single strand of dark brown, alternating the squares to give the background a checkered effect.

Patch #23: Countryside

MATERIALS
- Hand-dyed silk twist
- Pearsall's silk Filo-floss
- DMC embroidery floss
- Perle cotton, #3 weight

DESIGN AREA	STITCHES	Amount	Color
		SILK TWIST	
First hill	Slanted Gobelin stitch	1 yard	green
		SILK FILO-FLOSS	
Second hill	Straight Gobelin stitch	2 yards	#84 green
		EMBROIDERY FLOSS	
Third hill	Vertical brick stitch	2 yards	#3013 light green
Fourth hill	Basketweave stitch	3 yards	#937 dark green
		PERLE COTTON	
House front and side	Horizontal brick stitch	5 yards	#918 brick
Gables	Straight Gobelin stitch	*	#918 brick
		SILK TWIST	
Door	Basketweave stitch	2 yards	peach
Roof	Encroaching Gobelin stitch	*	peach
Shutters	Straight Gobelin stitch	*	peach
Corner	Straight Gobelin stitch	*	peach
Windows	Straight Gobelin stitch	1 yard	cream

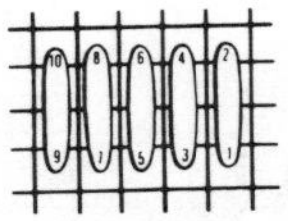

GOBELIN STITCH

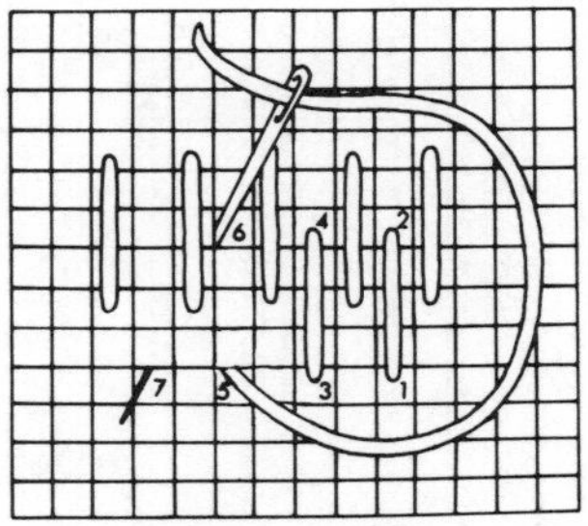

BRICK STITCH

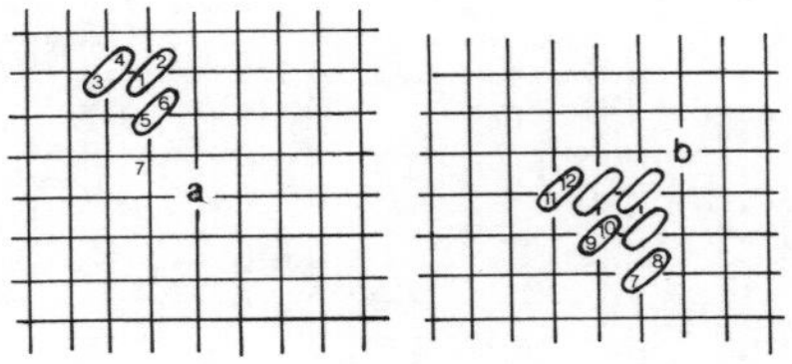

BASKETWEAVE STITCH

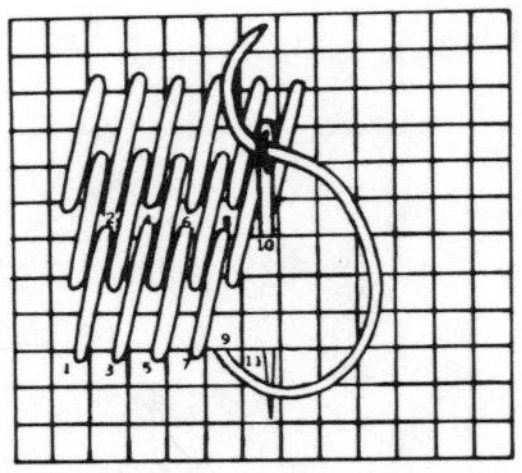

ENCROACHING GOBELIN

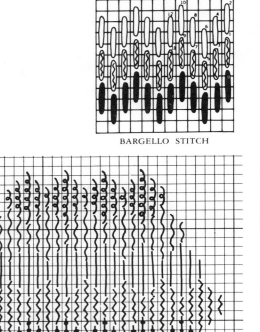

BARGELLO STITCH

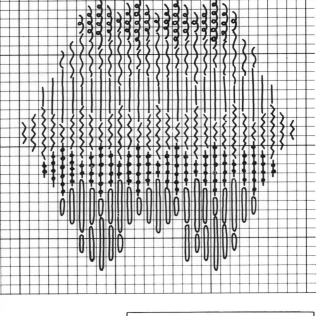

	EMBROIDERY FLOSS		
Tree trunk	Encroaching Gobelin stitch	1 yard	#632 brown
Tree leaves (in order from trunk upward)	Bargello stitch	½ yard	#935 dark green
		½ yard	#3053 medium green
		½ yard	#3013 pale green
		½ yard	#738 pale gold
		½ yard	#422 medium gold
		½ yard	#437 gold

* Use remainder of yarn from other design areas.

Graph Color Key

0	#935 DARK GREEN
⦂	#3053 MEDIUM GREEN
⧹	#3013 PALE GREEN
∣	#738 PALE GOLD
2	#422 MEDIUM GOLD
3	#437 GOLD

INSTRUCTIONS
first hill
Use a single strand of green silk twist and work a slanted Gobelin stitch to fill in the hill area.

second hill
Use a full strand of green silk floss and work a long straight Gobelin stitch in a vertical direction to fill the hill area. Work over twice.

third hill
Use a full strand of green floss and work a vertical brick stitch over two threads to fill in the hill area.

fourth hill
Use a full strand of dark green floss and work a basketweave stitch to fill in the hill area.

house
In a single strand of brick Perle cotton, work the front and side of the house in a horizontal brick stitch over three threads. Work the gables in a straight Gobelin stitch. Use a single strand of peach silk twist for the door in a basketweave stitch. Work the roof in encroaching Gobelin

over three threads. Work the shutters in straight Gobelin. Work the corners in Gobelin over a single thread. Fill in the windows with a full strand of cream floss in a straight Gobelin stitch.

tree

Use a full strand of brown floss and work an encroaching Gobelin stitch to fill in the trunk. Work the leaves from the bottom to the top in the bargello rhythm shown on the graph.

Patch #25: Rainbow

MATERIALS
Mohair knitting
Hand-dyed silk twist
Perle cotton, #3 weight

SATIN STITCH

DESIGN AREA	STITCHES	MOHAIR KNITTING YARN	
		Amount	*Color*
Cloud	Satin stitch	10 yards	white
		SILK TWIST	
Cloudy sky (under cloud)	Encroaching oblique stitch	*	sand
Lower right sky	Encroaching oblique stitch	*	blue
Rain drops (over cloudy sky)	Running stitch	*	blue
Rainbow (in order top to bottom)	Encroaching Gobelin stitch	5 yards	yellow

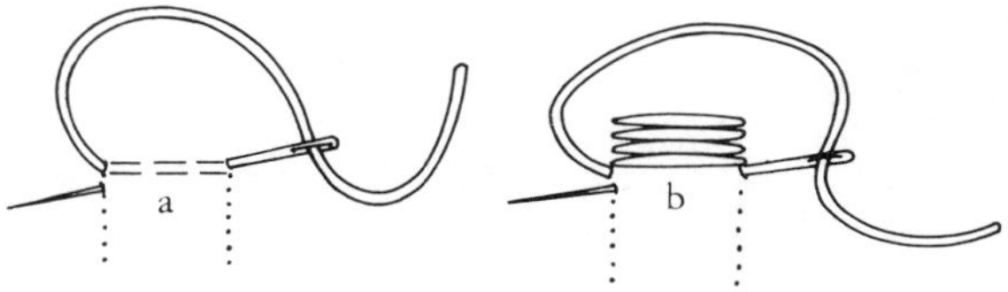

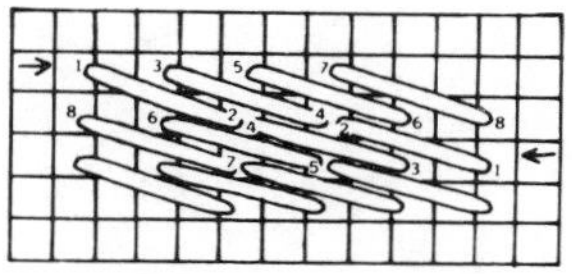

ENCROACHING OBLIQUE STITCH

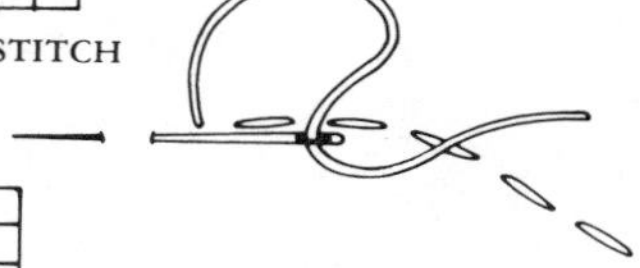

RUNNING STITCH

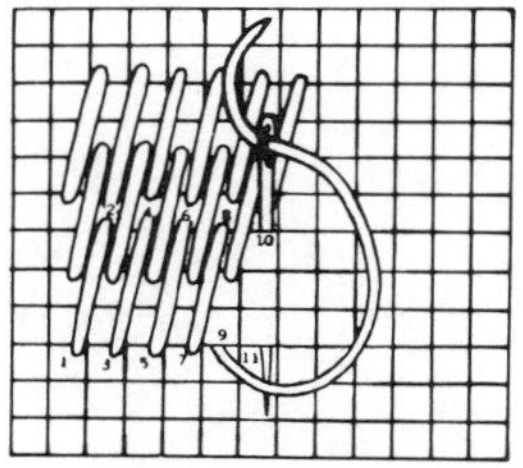

ENCROACHING GOBELIN

1 yard	pink
7 yards	sand
1 yard	pale green
1 yard	lavender
7 yards	blue

PERLE COTTON

Background	Encroaching oblique stitch	10 yards	pale blue
(from top of cloud			
to edge of patch)			

* Use remainder of yarn from other design areas

INSTRUCTIONS

With a double strand of mohair yarn, use a satin stitch to fill in the cloud area. Repeat twice for fullness. With a single strand of sand silk twist, work the cloudy sky in an encroaching oblique stitch over four threads. Finish the lower sky in a single strand of pale blue silk twist in an encroaching oblique stitch. With the same blue yarn, use a running stitch over three threads to work the rain drops, in a vertical direction. For the rainbow, work with a single strand of silk twist and use an encroaching Gobelin stitch over five threads in the following colors: yellow, pink, sand, pale green, lavender, and blue. Fill in the area from the top of the cloud to the top of the rainbow with yellow silk twist using an encroaching oblique stitch. The upper sky is worked in a single strand of blue Perle cotton in an encroaching oblique stitch over four threads.

Rabbit

STITCHES

Satin stitch: rabbit body and tail   Loop stitch: radishes
French knot: eye

MATERIALS

Striated silk   Mohair knitting wool
    3 yards natural $\frac{1}{2}$ yard white

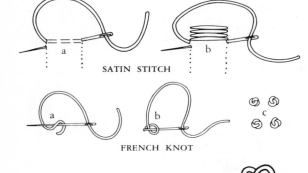

SATIN STITCH

FRENCH KNOT

LOOP STITCH

INSTRUCTIONS

Work a single strand of natural silk yarn in a satin stitch for each section of the rabbit, thereby defining "lines" to show his legs, body, and head. Repeat again for fullness. Work the tail in mohair yarn and a satin stitch. Repeat 4 times for a fluffy effect. Add a single red floss French knot for his eye and a few green loop stitches for his stolen radishes!

FINISHING THE QUILT

Remove the needlework from the working frame and block it front side up to preserve the texture and fragile stitchery. Pin the moiré ribbon to the edge of the needlework. Miter the corners for a picture frame effect. Machine stitch in place, as close to the needlework edge as possible. On the muslin backing, draw an outline of the patches and title them (for future generations may be curious) in indelible pen or hard lead pencil. Cut the muslin $\frac{1}{2}$ inch larger than the canvas and turn this edge under; blind stitch it in place. You may choose to embroider a favorite quotation around the four edges of the moiré ribbon, or include it on the back with your titles and personal data. Sew the three curtain loops in place for a balanced wall-hanging.

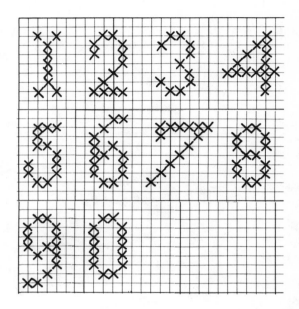

VARIATIONS ON A THEME

The personal patchwork quilt can become an album cover. The family motto or a favorite quotation worked in embroidery into the ribbon framework can make it an heirloom tapestry.

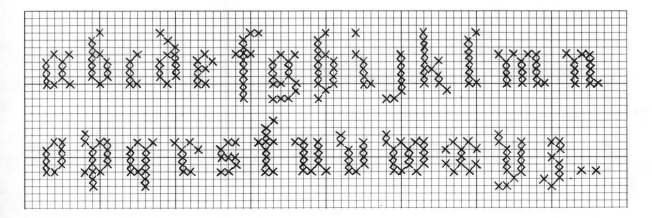

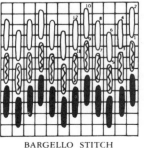

DEXTERITY: Level I

MATERIALS

Tapestry needle #20

Mono canvas #12, 12 by 15 inches

DMC cotton tapestry #4, for rainbow and background

DMC embroidery floss, for letters and details

$\frac{1}{4}$ yard narrow velvet ribbon

Plywood, $\frac{1}{4}$ inch thick for mounting

Frame, $9\frac{1}{2}$ by $13\frac{1}{2}$ inches

DESIGN AREA	STITCHES	COTTON TAPESTRY YARN	
		Amount	*Color*
Rainbow	Bargello stitch	1 skein	#2753 violet
		1 skein	#2328 violet
		1 skein	#2398 violet
		1 skein	#2798 blue
		1 skein	#2799 blue
		1 skein	#2800 blue

BARGELLO STITCH

		1 skein	#2469 green
		1 skein	#2471 green
		1 skein	#2472 green
		1 skein	#2745 yellow
		1 skein	#2727 yellow
		1 skein	#2726 yellow
		1 skein	#2354 red
		1 skein	#2303 red
		1 skein	#2753 red
Background	Continental stitch	7 skeins	ecru

EMBROIDERY FLOSS

Letters			
HAPPINESS	Cross-stitch	1 skein	# 351 red
CREATES ITS OWN	Cross-stitch	1 skein	# 519 blue
Sun	French knots	1 skein	# 783 dark gold
		1 skein	# 725 medium gold
		1 skein	# 744 light gold
Rain drops	Running stitch	*	# 519 blue

* Use remainder of yarn from other design areas.

CONTINENTAL STITCH

CROSS-STITCH

FRENCH KNOT

RUNNING STITCH

SPECIAL HINTS

Staple the canvas to a working frame. Handle cotton tapestry yarn with care; it tends to fuzz and pill with excessive handling.

Finished piece is 14 inches wide and 10 inches high.

INSTRUCTIONS
rainbow

Use a single strand of cotton tapestry yarn, and work a bargello stitch. The bargello rhythm is: over four threads with a step of two. Work one stitch 12 times; two stitches 13 times; three stitches 10 times; four stitches 6 times; five stitches 6 times; eight stitches 1 time; fourteen stitches 1 time. Build each row upon this one. Start at the bottom

with light violet #2753, and work toward the top in the order listed in the chart.

background
Use a single strand of ecru cotton tapestry yarn, and make a continental stitch. Work from edges of the rainbow to the outer canvas.

letters
Use two strands pulled from the six strands of embroidery floss, and work a cross-stitch. Follow the graph for the scale and shape of the letters.

sun
Using a sharp needle to penetrate the background stitches and a full six strands of embroidery floss, work French knots from the inside dark section to the lighter outside section. Mass the stitches together for a dense effect. Use the medium gold #725 and work long straight stitches for the rays of the sun.

rain
Use a full six strands of embroidery floss and make a running stitch in a random pattern to create rain drops.

FINISHING
Block the canvas in the traditional manner. Cut a $2\frac{1}{2}$ inch strip from the velvet ribbon, and attach in place with blind stitches near the bottom of the rainbow. Tie a bow, using the remainder of the velvet ribbon, and tack it in place on the velvet strip. Mount the canvas on $\frac{1}{4}$-inch plywood, staple, and frame.

VARIATIONS ON A THEME
With its happiness and sunshine, the rainbow makes a fine pillow or an insert for a serving tray. Be sure to check dimensions before you start and adjust where necessary.

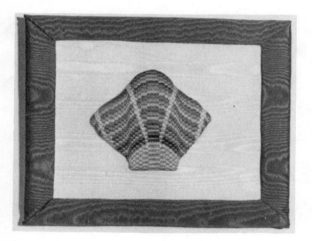

DEXTERITY: Level II

STITCHES
    Bargello stitch: seashell

MATERIALS
    Tapestry needle #22
    Mono canvas #18, 6 by 9 inches
    DMC Mouline embroidery floss
        1 skein ecru
        2 skeins #351 coral (deep)
        2 skeins #352 coral (medium)
        2 skeins #353 coral (light)
    One photo mat board, 10 by 12 inches
    Ivory moiré background fabric, 10 by 12 inches
    Coral moiré frame fabric, 14 by 16 inches
    Small portion of polyester fiberfill for stuffing
    Scrap of fabric, 6 inches by 7 inches, for backing
    Curved upholstery needle

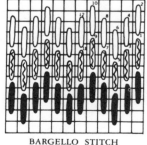

BARGELLO STITCH

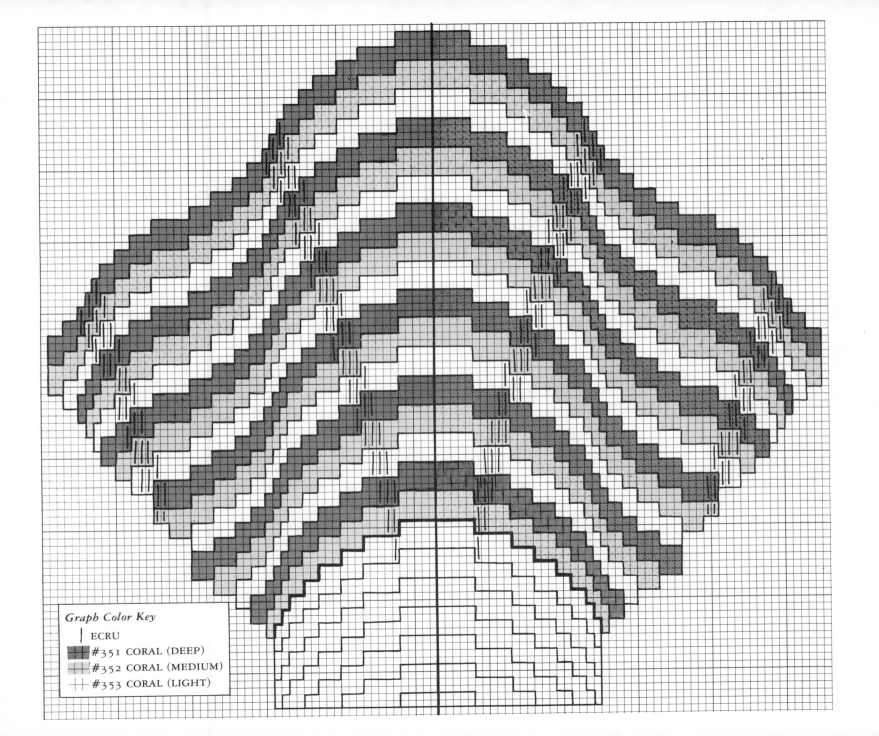

Graph Color Key

| ECRU

#351 CORAL (DEEP)

#352 CORAL (MEDIUM)

#353 CORAL (LIGHT)

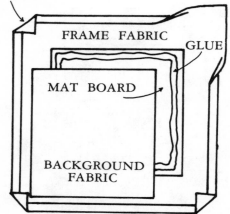

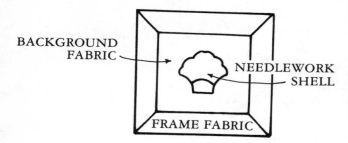

SPECIAL HINTS

If you are unable to find moiré fabric, any suitable fabric, such as taffeta, can be substituted. However, a thick fabric will be too bulky for the frame; a medium weight fabric is best.

Finished piece is 12 inches wide and 10 inches high.

INSTRUCTIONS

Cut the embroidery floss into 18-inch lengths, and separate all strands. Make a working thread of nine strands, and use a bargello stitch. The bargello rhythm is over four threads with a step of two. Follow the graph for shape and shading.

FINISHING

Stay stitch around the entire edge of the shell, as close to the needlework as possible; trim the excess canvas to within $\frac{1}{4}$ inch. Cut a scrap of fabric, approximately 6 by 7 inches, for the shell backing. With right sides together, sew all around the outer edge of the shell; round off the square edge of the stitches where they protrude. Slit the center back of the lining, and turn the shell right side out. Press the edges flat with your fingers. Topstitch the base of the shell as shown. Stuff the remainder of the shell with a small amount of fiberfill, and whipstitch the back opening closed.

Place the shell in the center of the background fabric, and tack it in place with small stitches at the corners, base, and top of the shell only, so that it remains puffy. Glue the background fabric to the photo mat board. Place the glue only where it will not show, that is, behind the shell and along the outer edges of the piece which will be covered by the fabric frame. Fold the raw fabric edges in $\frac{1}{2}$ inch and press. With the mat board centered, fold the frame fabric toward the center, mitering the corners. Pin in place while adding a small portion of fiberfill to give the frame a curve. A curved upholstery needle is best for sewing the frame. Use matching thread and small blind stitches. Sew a small curtain loop at the center back for hanging.

VARIATIONS ON A THEME

The shell can also be a potpourri pillow with a small pocket in the back for personal messages, or a private jewelry cache.

Thistle

DEXTERITY: Level I

STITCHES
> Continental stitch: stem and leaves
> Satin stitch: thistle
> Elongated French knots: petals

MATERIALS
> Tapestry needle #20
> Disposable canvas, 6 inches square
> Paternayan 3-ply Persian
>> 4 strands #915 light green
>> 6 strands #910 medium green
>> 1 strand #618 lavender
>> 1 strand #612 purple
>
> 1 yard angora or mohair
> Working frame, 8 by 8 inches
> Piece of velvet fabric, 11 inches square, for background
> Felt to back finished frame, 8 inches square

CONTINENTAL STITCH

SATIN STITCH

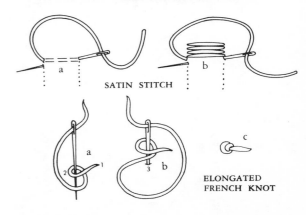

ELONGATED
FRENCH KNOT

SPECIAL HINTS

Wrap the background fabric around the working frame, and staple it to the back of the frame. Place the disposable canvas at the center of the fabric, and baste around the edges. Work the pattern from top to bottom. Start the continental stitch 2 inches from the top frame edge.

Finished piece is 8 inches wide and 8 inches high.

INSTRUCTIONS

stem and leaves

Use 3-ply Persian wool, and work a continental stitch. Follow the graph. Remove the waste canvas by pulling it away from the needlework, thread by thread.

flower

Use a single strand separated from the 3-ply Persian wool, and work a satin stitch. Work the first row in purple, then lavender; top with angora in between, letting the purple and lavendar show through. Shape according to the graph.

petals

Use a single strand of angora yarn, and work a few elongated French knots. Place them at random.

FINISHING

Glue the felt square to the back of the working frame. Attach a picture hanger on the back at top center.

VARIATIONS ON A THEME

The whimsical thistle can become a pocket or a yoke on a dress or blouse. When lined with appropriate materials, it can become a glasses case. With a zipper closure, it can be a small change purse.

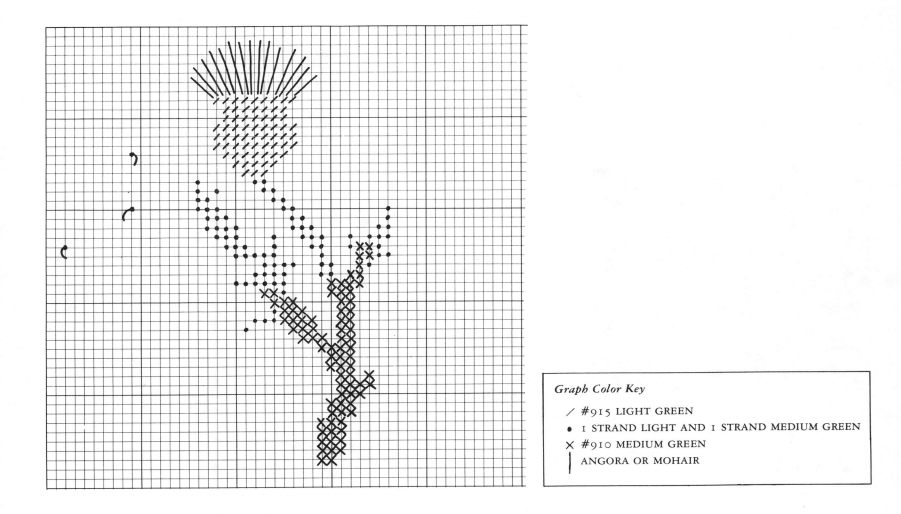

Graph Color Key

/ #915 LIGHT GREEN
• I STRAND LIGHT AND I STRAND MEDIUM GREEN
X #910 MEDIUM GREEN
| ANGORA OR MOHAIR

175

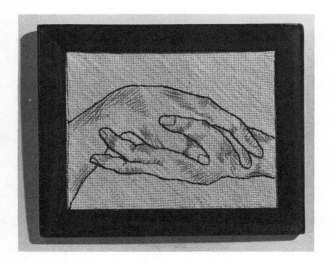

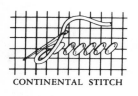

CONTINENTAL STITCH

BACKSTITCH

DEXTERITY: Level III

STITCHES
    Continental stitch: background
    Backstitch: outline of hands
    Straight stitch: sketch lines

MATERIALS
    Tapestry needle #18
    Embroidery needle #10
    Penelope canvas #10, 9 by 11 inches
    Fawcett linen 10/5 weight
        5 skeins peach (15 yards each)
    DMC Mouline embroidery floss
        1 skein #356 light umber
        1 skein #355 burnt umber
    Picture frame, 7 by 9 inches
    Plywood, $\frac{1}{4}$ inch thick, cut to fit frame

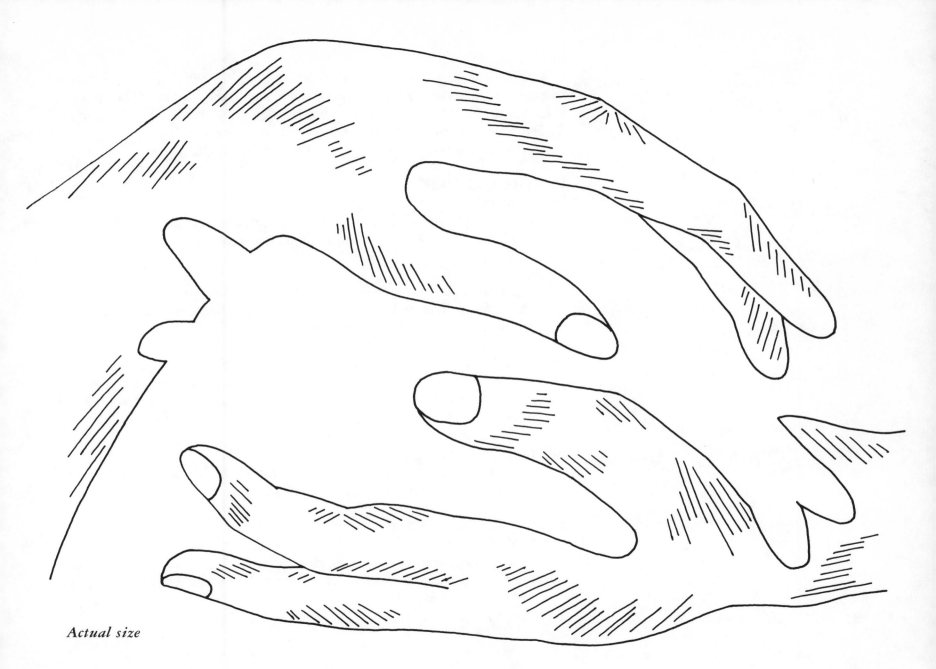

Actual size

SPECIAL HINTS

Trace the outline of the picture-frame opening onto the canvas. Use a working frame so the canvas does not warp; staple the canvas in place. Linen yarn has a natural striation when dyed which should not be considered a defect; it adds depth and character to your needlework.

Finished piece is 9 inches wide and 7 inches high.

INSTRUCTIONS
background

Use a single strand of linen, and work a continental stitch. Work the stitch a few rows beyond the lines of the frame opening.

hands

Trace the hands onto the paper, and cut each one out separately. Trace the hand outline with a light pencil onto the needlework background. An embroidery needle is recommended to execute the embroidered hands. Use a full six strands of burnt umber and a backstitch to outline both hands. For the sketch lines, use a single strand pulled from the six-strand light-umber embroidery floss, and work a straight stitch. Use the illustration as a guide to the placement of stitches; vary the size and density for the proper effect.

FINISHING

Remove the canvas from the working frame, and block in the traditional manner. Staple to $\frac{1}{4}$-inch plywood cut to the proper size for your picture frame.

VARIATIONS ON A THEME

With the addition of names and dates—either embroidered or worked into the needlepoint background—this project makes a lovely and lasting wedding or anniversary gift. (See graphed alphabets, pages 119 and 165, and numerals, page 165.)

Vest

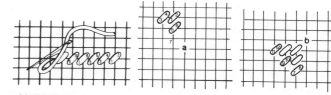

DEXTERITY: Level III

STITCHES
    Continental stitch: flowers
    Basketweave stitch: background

MATERIALS
    Tapestry needle #22
    Mono canvas #18, ⅔ yard by 24 inches wide
    French wool, for background
        2 hanks (8 skeins, 100 strands each) #122 plum
    DMC Mouline embroidery floss
        leaves
            4 skeins #3348 light green
            6 skeins #3347 medium green
            5 skeins #3345 dark green
        blue flowers
            2 skeins #928 light blue
            2 skeins #926 medium blue
            2 skeins #924 dark blue

CONTINENTAL STITCH   BASKETWEAVE STITCH

pink flowers
>7 skeins #225 light pink
>
>8 skeins #224 medium pink
>
>4 skeins #221 dark pink

gold flowers
>2 skeins #746 light gold
>
>2 skeins #407 medium gold
>
>2 skeins #632 dark gold

Vest pattern without front darts

$\frac{2}{3}$ yard velvet fabric for vest back, 36 inches wide

$\frac{2}{3}$ yard suitable fabric for lining, 45 inches wide

5 hook fasteners for front closure

SPECIAL HINTS

Since this project is a duplication of an heirloom, the yarn and materials are an estimate. Be generous when you purchase your supplies. It is wise to work the large floral sections first, then the smaller sections; work the background last. For the best fit, choose a pattern which has no front darts but has darts in the back. Adapt your needlework to the front pattern pieces by tracing the front vest pattern pieces onto your canvas. Do not include the seam allowance; trace along the seam line, and work your needlepoint to that line.

INSTRUCTIONS
flowers

Work the flowers first, with a full six strands of DMC floss and using a continental stitch. Start at the top of a floral section, and work down. Finish one color section before starting another; that is, one blue flower, then a pink flower, etc. It is helpful when changing yarn shades so often (light, medium, dark), to have several needles threaded, and to work across the row, rather than skipping all over the design with one shade. You will be less likely to make mistakes this way. Follow the graph. The placement of the floral arrangements is at your discretion. You may wish to use only the small designs if you are making it for a small person; or

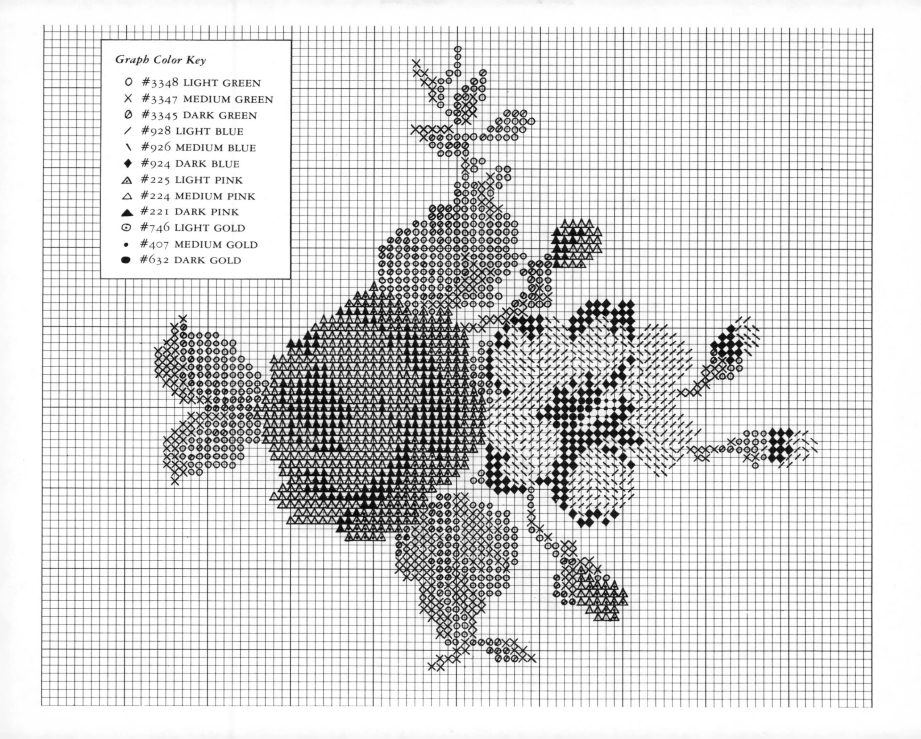

Graph Color Key

O	#3348	LIGHT GREEN
X	#3347	MEDIUM GREEN
Ø	#3345	DARK GREEN
/	#928	LIGHT BLUE
\	#926	MEDIUM BLUE
◆	#924	DARK BLUE
△	#225	LIGHT PINK
△	#224	MEDIUM PINK
▲	#221	DARK PINK
⊙	#746	LIGHT GOLD
•	#407	MEDIUM GOLD
◖	#632	DARK GOLD

you may wish to use one design and repeat the motif throughout the needlework piece. This is your heirloom, so make it to suit your taste and your dimensions!

background

With three strands of French wool #122, work the background in a basketweave stitch; this will give longer wear and produce less distortion of your canvas than the continental stitch will. Start work at the upper right corner of the shoulders and work across in a diagonal direction, around the flowers.

FINISHING

Block the needlework and trim the excess canvas to within $\frac{1}{2}$ inch of the needlework. Follow the sewing instructions included with your pattern. Treat your needlework as fabric, but treat it tenderly. Decorative hook fasteners are recommended for a closure because they will not puncture the needlework. Plain sewing hooks can also be used; then add a cord for lacing.

Weathervane

DEXTERITY: Level III

STITCH

Encroaching oblique

MATERIALS

Tapestry needle #22
Mono canvas #18, 11 by 26 inches
Copper embroidery thread, 5 skeins (3-ply)
Working frame, 12 by 26 inches
4-ounce bottle of hydrogen peroxide
Photo mat board, 20 by 30 inches
Jar of copper enamel paint ($\frac{1}{3}$ ounce)

SPECIAL HINTS

Finished piece is 11 inches high and 23 inches long.

ENCROACHING OBLIQUE STITCH

INSTRUCTIONS

Trace the design outline onto the canvas, and mount the canvas on the working frame. Cut the thread into 27-inch lengths. Use a triple strand, and

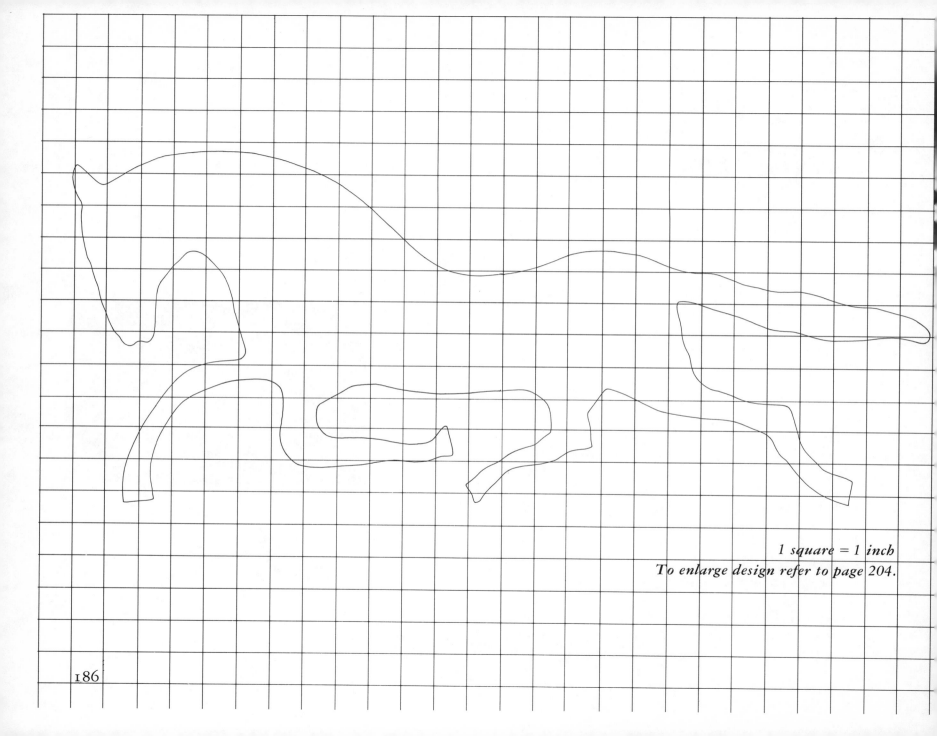

1 square = 1 inch
To enlarge design refer to page 204.

work an encroaching oblique stitch over four threads. Move the position of the thread through the needle several times while working to avoid fraying the copper coating. Start at the head and work toward the legs.

FINISHING

Apply several coats of peroxide to different areas of the horse with a paint brush until the desired look of "aging" is achieved. Let the needlework dry between coats to avoid saturation of the canvas. Remove the needlework from the working frame, and trim excess canvas to within $\frac{1}{4}$ inch. Fold the raw edges of the canvas to the back, and glue them in place; clip the curves to make folding them easier. Using the finished needlework as a pattern, trace the outline onto the photo mat board. Cut the mat board with a razor-edged knife or sharp scissors, and sand the rough edges. Glue the needlework to the mat board, and let it dry under some heavy objects so that it will remain flat. Be sure the mat board does not extend beyond the needlework. Use copper paint to touch up any raw canvas spots and to cover the raw edge of the mat board. Hang by glue-on picture hooks at the head and rump.

DEXTERITY: Level II

MATERIALS

Tapestry needle #22
Mono canvas #18, 11 by 14 inches
Fawcett linen yarn 10/5 and 20/2 weights } Cathedral
DMC Perle Cotton, #3 weight
DMC embroidery floss

Tapestry needle #22
Mono canvas #18, 11 by 14 inches
Pearsall's silk Filo-floss } Window
DMC embroidery floss
1 hank grey glass beads

$1\frac{1}{4}$ yards $\frac{7}{8}$-inch wide grey grosgrain ribbon
$\frac{1}{2}$ yard $\frac{3}{4}$-inch wide grey grosgrain ribbon
1 felt square, 9 by 12 inches
Stretcher frame, 9 by 12 inches

DESIGN AREA	STITCHES	LINEN YARN	
		Color	*Amount*
Cathedral	Brick stitch	natural (10/5 weight)	4 skeins
		natural (20/2 weight)	4 skeins
		light grey (10/5 weight)	4 skeins
		light grey (20/2 weight)	4 skeins
		PERLE COTTON	
Fretwork	Long-armed cross-stitch, French stitch, and leaf stitch	#840 brown	1 skein
		EMBROIDERY FLOSS	
	Straight Gobelin stitch	#841 brown	
		PEARSALL'S SILK FILO-FLOSS	
Window	Straight Gobelin stitch	#99D dark red	3 skeins
		#99A flame red	3 skeins
		#156 gold	3 skeins
		# 44 blue	3 skeins
		#121A purple	3 skeins
		EMBROIDERY FLOSS	
Outline	Straight Gobelin stitch	#535 grey	2 skeins

BRICK STITCH

LONG-ARMED CROSS-STITCH

KNOTTED (FRENCH) STITCH

LEAF STITCH

GOBELIN STITCH

SPECIAL HINTS

Outline a 9- by 12-inch space on the center of the canvas. Trace the outline of the doorway 1¾ inches from the right outline edge. A "Scotch" method was used for the stained glass window to defray the cost of silk materials. If you choose to use the standard Gobelin, double the quantity of silk purchased.

Finished piece is 9 inches wide and 12 inches high.

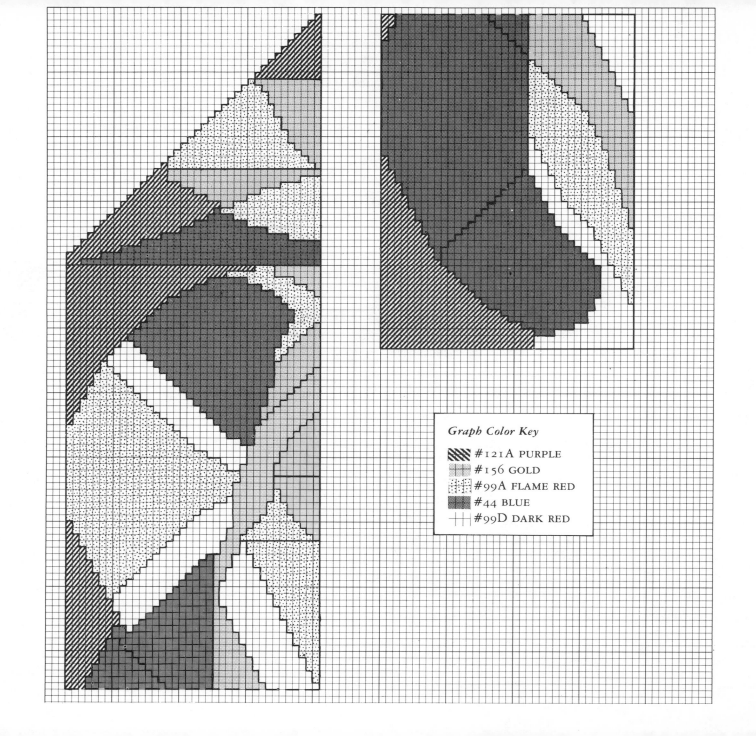

Graph Color Key

▨	#121A PURPLE
▦	#156 GOLD
▨	#99A FLAME RED
▨	#44 BLUE
▦	#99D DARK RED

INSTRUCTIONS
cathedral

Use a single strand of 10/5 heavy weight linen in grey and natural alternately with two strands of 20/2 light weight linen (one strand of grey, one natural together). Start at the bottom left corner in a brick stitch to simulate cobblestones. Work the yarn colors at random for a mottled effect. Follow the outline edges and doorway. Increase one hole for each row to form the peak; decrease in the same proportion down the other side.

fretwork

Sides. First row: Use a single strand of Perle cotton, and work a long-armed cross-stitch over three canvas threads. Second row: Use a double strand of DMC embroidery floss, and work a straight Gobelin stitch over two canvas threads. Third row: Use a single strand of Perle cotton, and work a long-armed cross-stitch over two canvas threads.

Bottom. Use a single strand of Perle cotton, and work a long-armed cross-stitch over three canvas threads.

Peak. Use a single strand of Perle cotton, and work a leaf stitch at both corners at the top. First row: Use nine strands of DMC embroidery floss, and work a straight Gobelin stitch over three canvas threads. Second row: Use nine strands of DMC embroidery floss, and work a straight Gobelin stitch over five canvas threads, filling in the spaces at the center of the leaf, as shown. Third row: Use a single strand of Perle cotton, and work a French stitch over four canvas threads; elongate the stitches at the top, as shown.

window

Begin work on the window pattern on the second piece of canvas $1\frac{3}{4}$ inches from the right canvas edge. Use a single strand of Filo-floss, and work a straight Gobelin stitch. Follow the color graph. Start at the top of the design and work down. Handle the silk thread carefully as it tends to fray; keep your working threads short, and use beeswax for ease in handling. Use a single strand #535 DMC floss, and work a straight Gobelin stitch over twelve threads, in a horizontal direction, to outline the entire edge of the completed silk window so the canvas will not show.

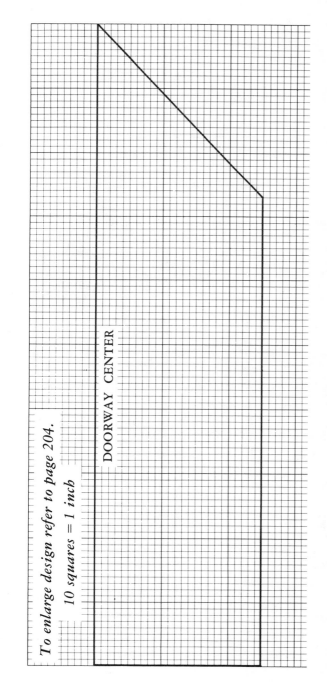

To enlarge design refer to page 204.

10 squares = 1 inch

DOORWAY CENTER

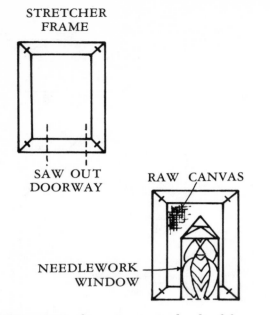

STRETCHER
FRAME

SAW OUT
DOORWAY

RAW CANVAS

NEEDLEWORK
WINDOW

Mount window canvas to back of frame

NEEDLEWORK
CATHEDRAL

COVER OUTSIDE
EDGES WITH
WIDE GROSGRAIN

NARROW
GROSGRAIN

lead seams

Remove the beads from the string; place in small bowl. Use a beading needle and a single strand of #535 DMC floss, doubled over and knotted at one end. Place the beads on the needle one at a time until the length of the beads equals that of the seam you wish to cover. Work various numbers of beads according to the size of each seam. If the seam is long, take a few tacking stitches to hold the beads in place. Stitch the beads along the seam line in between the colors to simulate lead seams.

FINISHING

Trim the canvas inside the cathedral doorway to within $\frac{1}{4}$ inch of needlework; fold it back and glue it in place. Mark the sides of the cathedral doorway on the wooden frame. Saw out the center section of the front. Glue the frame corners to secure in place. Mount the canvas on a 9- by 12-inch frame with a staple gun. Trim the window canvas to 9 by 12 inches, and mount it to the back of the cathedral frame with a staple gun. Cover the outside edge of the frame and the raw cathedral canvas with *wide* grosgrain ribbon, and cover the inside edge of the frame and the bottom canvas edge with *narrow* grosgrain ribbon, gluing the ribbon in place. Cover the back of the window canvas with a 9- by 12-inch felt square, and glue it in place. Hang with a metal picture hanger at the center top of the frame.

VARIATIONS ON A THEME

Xmas makes an excellent holiday center piece for your table. When photographed in color, it becomes a unique Christmas card.

Yoke

DEXTERITY: Level III

STITCHES
    French knots: buds
    Whipped spider web: cornflower
    Bullion stitch: marigold
    Lazy daisy stitch: daisy, leaves
    Raised cup stitch: morning glory
    Threaded running stitch: border
    Cross-stitch: border
    Cretan stitch: border

MATERIALS
    Tapestry needle #22
    Ecru mono canvas #18, 6 by 9 inches
    DMC cotton embroidery floss
        2 skeins #677 pale yellow
        1 skein #334 blue
        1 skein #744 deep yellow

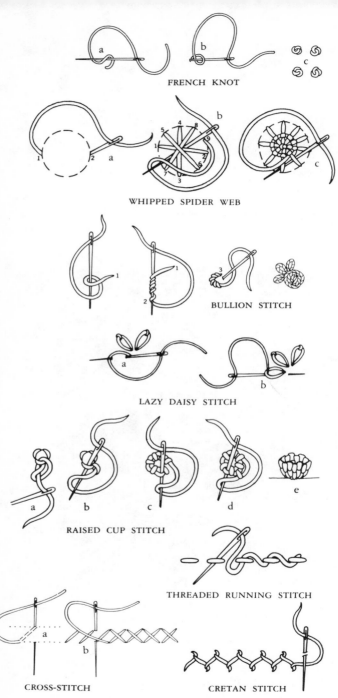

FRENCH KNOT

WHIPPED SPIDER WEB

BULLION STITCH

LAZY DAISY STITCH

RAISED CUP STITCH

THREADED RUNNING STITCH

CROSS-STITCH

CRETAN STITCH

1 skein #368 light green
1 skein #519 aqua
1 skein #320 deep green
DMC Perle cotton #3 weight
1 skein #800 light blue
Pattern for child's floor-length dress with a yoke
2½ yards floral fabric
2½ yards ecru lace, ½ inch wide
7½ yards ecru lace, ¾ inch wide
1½ yards grosgrain ribbon, ¼ inch wide
3 yards grosgrain ribbon, ⅝ inch wide
3 yards grosgrain ribbon, 1½ inches wide

SPECIAL HINTS

Mark a 5- by 7½-inch rectangle on the canvas, with a dot at each corner to form a frame. Space the rows of needlework border one canvas thread apart. Instead of having background stitchery, the canvas is left open. Be sure to hide your raw threads behind the needlework to keep the background canvas open.

Finished needlework piece is 5½ inches wide and 8¼ inches high.

INSTRUCTIONS

border sides and bottom

With six strands of embroidery floss #677 pale yellow, work one row of Cretan stitch over four threads around the entire rectangle frame. Use two strands of floss #519 aqua and a cross-stitch over two threads; work one row on each side. Work another row of Cretan stitches on each side with #677.

border top

For rows 1, 3, 5, use six strands of floss #334 blue, and work running stitches two threads apart. Thread the running stitches with a single strand of Perle cotton #800 light blue. Cross-stitch rows 2 and 4 in the same manner as the sides. For the last row, use Cretan stitches, as above.

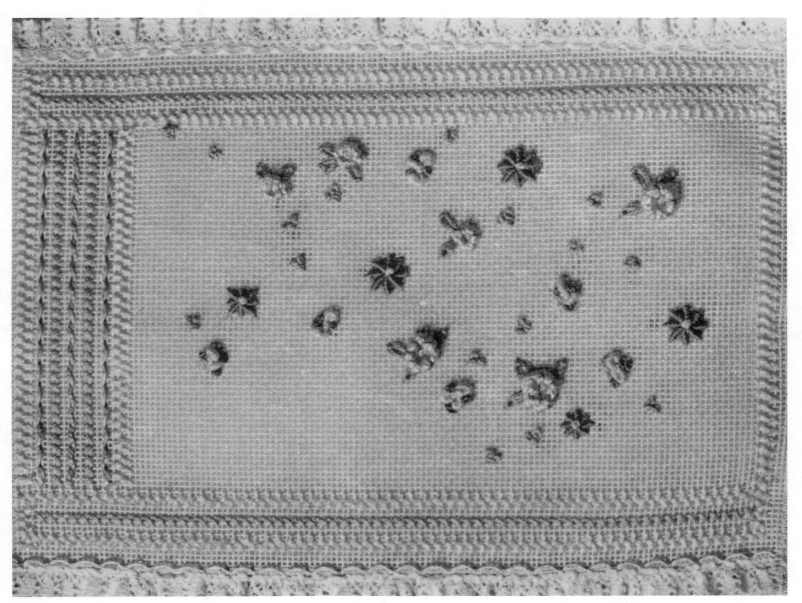

Actual size

center

Scatter the flowers at random, balancing the size and color at your discretion. Place the five blue whipped spider web/French knot flowers first, since this is the strongest color. Use six strands of floss #334 blue for the flower, and six strands of floss #774 deep yellow and one French knot for the center.

For the six raised cup flowers, the more rows worked, the larger the flower; vary the sizes. Use a single strand of Perle cotton #800 light blue for the flower, and six strands of floss #677 pale yellow and one French knot for the center. For the leaves, use six strands of floss #368 light green and a lazy daisy stitch.

For the six bullion flowers, use six strands of floss #677 pale yellow. Wrap the needle 6, 9, and 12 times for the petals, to vary the sizes; work three petals for each flower.

For the center, work a French knot in floss #744 deep yellow.

For the leaves, use six strands of floss #320 deep green and a few French knots.

For the buds, work sixteen groups of French knots; use floss #519 aqua. Form the buds by grouping three French knots together, and scatter them among the other flowers.

FINISHING

Trim the canvas to within $\frac{1}{2}$ inch of the needlework. Leave a border of three canvas threads on all sides of the needlework as part of the design. Treat the needlework section as a piece of fabric and join it to the dress following the pattern instructions for assembly. There will be approximately $\frac{1}{3}$ inch canvas seam allowance.

lining

Use the front bodice section as a pattern for the front bodice lining. Sew the lining to the bodice around the neckline, clipping curves at the corners. Turn it right side out and press. Fold the raw edge of the lining to the inside, and hemstitch in place.

trim

Hem the sleeves to the desired length. Topstitch the narrow ribbon and narrow lace 2 inches above the hemline, and the wider lace to the sleeve edge. Topstitch the narrow lace to both sides of the canvas yoke section.

Topstitch the wide lace and the narrow ribbon across the front bodice waistline to the side seams. For the sash, cut the wide ribbon into halves, each 1½ yards long; fold the raw edges under, and topstitch at the side seams. Hemstitch the raw ends of the sash to form a point. Hem the skirt to the desired length; topstitch the medium-width ribbon to the bottom edge and 3 inches above for a second row. Sew the wide lace to both sides of each ribbon row.

VARIATIONS ON A THEME

The yoke can become a billfold, a picture, a box cover.

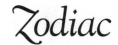

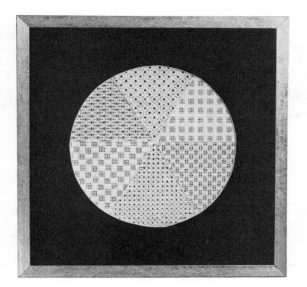

DEXTERITY: Level III

STITCHES

    Step stitch: section 1
    Basket stitch: section 2
    Diamond eyelet stitch: section 3
    Single fagoting: section 4
    Double stitch: section 5
    Wave stitch: section 6

MATERIALS

    Tapestry needle #24
    White mono canvas #14, 12 by 12 inches
        (should be of excellent quality to withstand the tension)
    Working frame, 12 inches
    1 ball white DMC Perle cotton #5, blanc neige
    3 skeins white DMC embroidery floss, blanc neige
    $\frac{1}{3}$ yard black suede cloth
    Small flashlight (optional)
    Frame, 12 by 12 inches

SPECIAL HINTS

Do not consider making this piece without a working frame. It is essential because the stitches must be pulled with extreme tension to create the lace effect.

Separate the embroidery floss by cutting it into equal lengths and slowly pulling each thread lengthwise, one at a time, through the strands of 6-ply floss. If the working strands break, you may have to take out a few stitches to have a tail long enough to weave into the back and begin again.

It is necessary to be aware of the direction and angle of the stitches in the pattern. The stitches must angle properly and the back cross-threads must not show through the open work.

Tension is the primary factor in this work, and you will find it helpful to use the side of your needle to ease the canvas threads prior to pulling it through. Do not be surprised if your needle breaks—it simply means you're pulling tightly. Keep a few extra needles on hand.

Finished piece, including frame, is 13 inches wide and 13 inches high.

STITCHES	YARN	START	TENSION	WORKING DIRECTION
1: Step stitch	Embroidery Floss	Center point	None	Diagonal rows
2: Basket stitch	Embroidery Floss	Lower right corner on outside line	None	All vertical rows, then horizontal
3: Diamond eyelet stitch	Perle Cotton #5	Center	Maximum	Diagonal rows of half stitches
4: Single fagot stitch	Perle Cotton #5	Upper right corner	Maximum	Diagonal rows with a one-half turn
5: Double stitch	Perle Cotton #5	Upper right corner	Maximum	Alternating, right to left then left to

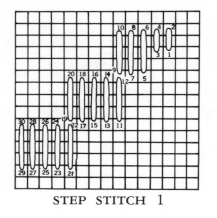

STEP STITCH 1

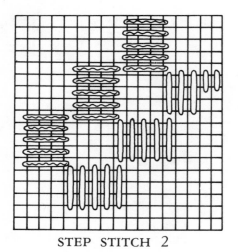

STEP STITCH 2

6: Wave stitch	Perle Cotton #5	Twelve horizontal threads below center point and in two vertical threads from straight edge	Maximum	right Alternating, right to left then left to right

INSTRUCTIONS

Assemble the working frame. Cut a 12-inch canvas square, and staple it at 2-inch intervals to the frame. With a hard-lead pencil, draw the 8¼-inch (in diameter) circle at the center of the back of the canvas. Divide the circle into six equal sections by first dividing the circle into halves and then dividing each half into thirds. Outline each section with sewing thread and a running stitch so the sections will show on the front side of the canvas. Note that the sections are not numbered consecutively around the circle. Follow the working order given below for ease of execution. Be sure to weave your thread into the back of the other stitches when crossing from one area to another, so they do not show through the open-weave canvas.

section 1: step stitch

Use nine strands of embroidery floss and work a step stitch. Start at the center point. Work five vertical satin stitches over four threads, then step down to the next five stitches, working in a diagonal row. The first and last stitch of each vertical and horizontal block of stitches occupy the same hole. For the next row, work in a horizontal direction in the same manner. Continue working in alternate vertical and horizontal rows. Use compensating stitches where necessary to conform to the triangular shape. Do not use any tension; be sure the strands of thread lie flat on the surface, not twisted, to give a uniform finish.

section 2: basket stitch

Use nine strands of embroidery floss and work a basket stitch over three threads. Start with vertical rows, beginning at the lower right corner at the outer line, four threads above the bottom edge. Work seven stitches, skip three threads, work ten stitches. Do not use any tension, but be sure the strands of thread lie flat on the surface, not twisted, to give a uniform finish. First stitch in vertical rows, back and forth; then in horizontal rows, back and forth. Note the subtle difference in shading between the vertical and horizontal stitches which adds a three-dimensional effect to this flat stitch. Sensational!

section 3: diamond eyelet

Use a single strand of Perle cotton #5, and work the diamond eyelet stitch over two and three threads as shown. Start at the center point with one diamond eyelet, and build rows of eyelets until the triangle shape is complete. Use compensating stitches where necessary to conform to the design. Pull very tightly on the center hole thread to open the eyelet. Keep the tension uniform so the eyelets will be the same size. Stitch in a diagonal direction making a series of half diamonds as shown. The other half of the diamonds will be completed on the return row.

section 4: single fagoting

Use a single strand of Perle cotton #5, and work a single fagot stitch over three threads. Rotate the canvas one-half a turn so the triangle is in the three o'clock position. Start at the upper right corner, and work a series of vertical stitches in a downward diagonal direction. Then rotate the canvas one-half a turn and repeat the same procedure.

In this procedure, the working method remains the same, but the angle of tension varies. Hence, you are pulling all the vertical stitches from bottom to top and pulling all the horizontal stitches from left to right. Pull very tightly so the two outer canvas threads are forced tightly against the center thread, thus creating the fagot.

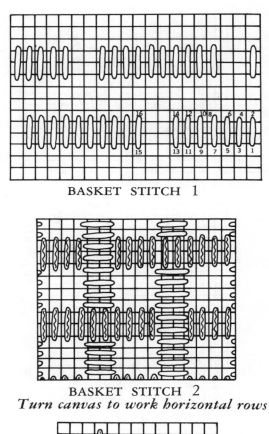

BASKET STITCH 1

BASKET STITCH 2
Turn canvas to work horizontal rows

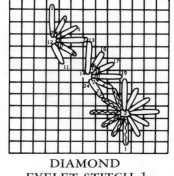

DIAMOND
EYELET STITCH 1
Work half diamonds first
Complete diamonds on return row

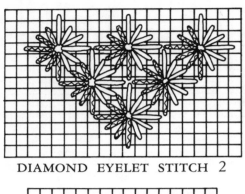

DIAMOND EYELET STITCH 2

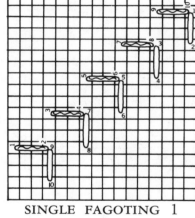

SINGLE FAGOTING 1

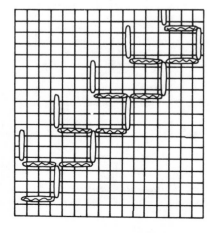

SINGLE FAGOTING 2

section 5: double stitch

Use a single strand of Perle cotton #5, and work a double stitch over five threads. Position the canvas with the basket stitch in the upper right corner. Start with the first row of double stitches overlapping the first and second basket strip by one thread. Thus, each straight double stitch will be centered on the basket stitch pattern.

Skip the first horizontal thread and follow the stitching sequence as illustrated in the graph. Complete the top row of double stitches after the remainder of the triangle is completed. Work from right to left, then back across from left to right, alternating rows until the triangle is complete. Pull the thread very tightly; the more tension, the more open and lacy the effect.

section 6: wave stitch

Use a single strand of Perle cotton #5, and work a wave stitch over four horizontal and two vertical threads. Start twelve threads below the center point and in two vertical threads. Two rows comprise one diamond-shaped stitch. Work the first row right to left, and the next row left to right. Continue alternating rows in order to angle the stitches in a proper position to create a wave pattern. Pull very tightly toward the left when working from right to left, and toward the right when working from left to right, to force the stitches from an angular to a vertical position.

It is necessary to weave in the working thread in the back of your needlework at the end of each row so you will equalize the tension and be able to place your needle in the proper position for the first stitch on the next row. Work the top of the diamond from top down to side, and work the bottom of the diamond from bottom up to side. Continue working $5\frac{1}{2}$ diamond rows toward the outer edge. Then rotate your project in the opposite direction and fill in the top of the triangle. Work compensating stitches where necessary.

FINISHING

Do *not* remove the needlework from the frame. Remove all the outline stitches of sewing thread. Use a single strand of Perle cotton #5, and make a single straight stitch to outline each pie-shaped piece within the circle. Cut a piece of suede cloth 12 inches square. On the wrong side of the fabric, mark the center. With a compass and a white pencil, draw an $8\frac{1}{8}$-inch circle on the wrong side of the fabric. Cut out the circle carefully, with precise edges. Center the cut-out circle of the fabric mat over the face of the needlework and glue in place.

Attach a 12-inch silver frame, overlapping the raw edges of canvas and suede cloth. For maximum dramatic effect, a small flashlight can be mounted with tape on the inside edge of the working frame. An additional strand of Perle cotton or crochet cotton may be glued to the outer edge of the circle—onto the suede cloth—for a more refined finish.

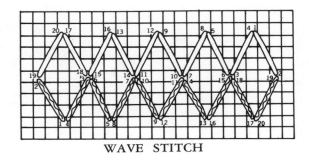

WAVE STITCH

VARIATIONS ON A THEME

Zodiac's pulled work technique can be used to make snow flakes. It can also be the focal point for a sampler or a fascinating mobile.

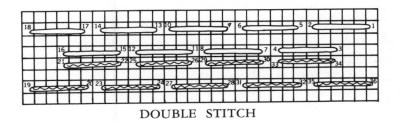

DOUBLE STITCH

Enlarging Designs

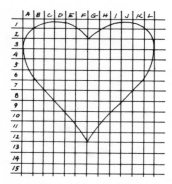

The reduced design

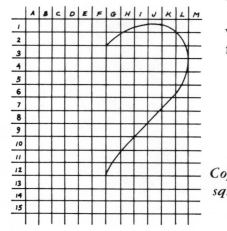

Copy the design square by square onto the larger grid

The easiest way to enlarge a design is to have it photostatted to full size. (You can locate a photostat service by looking in the Yellow Pages of your phone directory.)

Another method is to enlarge the design onto a grid of the proper size. For Album, Girl, Ocean, and Weathervane, copy the design square by square onto a one square per inch grid or one square per inch graph paper. For Doll and Xmas, copy the design square by square onto a ten squares per inch grid or ten squares per inch graph paper.

The square by square copying method is illustrated here. To determine what size paper you'll need for your enlarged design, refer to the size of the finished piece, given under Special Hints.

Needlework Schools and Collections

Needlework Schools

American Institute of Textile Arts, Pine Manor College, 400 Heath Street, Chestnut Hill, Massachusetts 02167

American School of Needlework, 464 Central Avenue, Northfield, Illinois 60093

Desert Needlework Ranch, 1645 North Harrison Road, Tuscon, Arizona 85715

Elsa Williams School of Needlework, West Townsend, Massachusetts 01474

Erica Wilson's School of Needlework, 717 Madison Avenue, New York, New York 10021

Nantucket School of Needlery, Textile Studios, Inc., The Windsor Mill, 121 Union Street, North Adams, Massachusetts 01247

Valentine Museum, 1015 East Clay Street, Richmond, Virginia 23219

Correspondence Schools

Embroider's Guild of America, 120 East 56th Street, New York, New York 10022

National Standards Council of American Embroiders, P.O. Box 4594, Pittsburgh, Pennsylvania 15205

MASSACHUSETTS
Deerfield Collections, Deerfield
Museum of Fine Arts, Boston
Old Sturbridge Village, Sturbridge

NEW YORK
Brooklyn Museum, Brooklyn
The Cloisters Collection, New York City
Cooper-Hewitt Museum of Design, New York City
Frick Collection, New York City
The Metropolitan Museum of Art, New York City
Museum of the City of New York, New York City

WASHINGTON, D.C.
National Cathedral
National Gallery
Textile Museum

OTHER CITIES
Art Institute of Chicago, Chicago, Illinois
Field Museum of Natural History, Chicago, Illinois
Connecticut Historical Society, Hartford, Connecticut
Museum of Fine Arts, Houston, Texas
Rhode Island School of Design, Providence, Rhode Island
Henry Francis du Pont Wenterthur Museum, Wenterthur, Delaware
Colonial Williamsburg, Williamsburg, Virginia
Statens Museum, Copenhagen, Denmark
Victoria and Albert Museum, London, England

AUTHOR'S NOTE
The above list is only a tease and far from complete. However, you may obtain the *Directory of Where to Find Embroidery and Other Textile Treasures in the U.S.A.* by ordering it prepaid ($2.50) from the National Standards Council of American Embroiders, P.O. Box 45105, Tulsa, Oklahoma 74145.

Suppliers

I can personally recommend the following suppliers for prompt and gracious service, as well as for expert advice.

All needlework materials (i.e. yarns, canvas, etc.) required for the projects within the book, can be found through these suppliers; other materials (glue, scissors, stapler, etc.) are considered standard household items. Frames, tacks, ribbons, etc., can be found at art supply stores or a sewing and notions department, unless otherwise stated within the instructions. If you live in a rural area, I suggest you write directly to the manufacturer for a list of local retail outlets, or order by mail.

Black Sheep, 48 Purchase Street, Rye, New York 10580:
Paternayan yarn
DMC embroidery floss (Mouline)
DMC cotton tapestry yarn
DMC wool tapestry yarn
DMC Perle cotton #3, #5
Disposable canvas

Blue Bead, 71 Church Street, Greenwich, Connecticut 06830:
Doll's chair
Domestic canvas
Nantucket yarns

Boutique Margot, 26 West 54th Street, New York, New York 10019:
Crewel yarn
DMC—entire line
Metallic threads
Swiss canvas
Silk floss
Silk twist
Assorted fine mesh canvases

Coulter Studio, 118 East 59th Street, New York, New York 10022:
Hand-spun yarn
Domestic linen
Natural dyed silk twist

Crafts Gallery, Ltd., 96 South Broadway, South Nyack, New York 10960:
Mail-order catalog and color cards available
DMC—entire line
Marlitt yarn
Bella Donna rayon yarn
Swedish linen yarn
Medici wool yarn
Au ver de soir (French silk yarn)
Domestic, imported, and disposable canvas

Selma's Art Needlework, 1645 Second Avenue (86th Street) New York, New York 10028:
Patterned cross-stitch canvas
Rayon yarns

German tapestry yarn
Imported stamped table linens
Rug canvas and wool

Sewmakers, 1619 Grand Avenue, Baldwin, New York 11510
Perforated paper

The Wooly End, 41 William Street, Greenwich, Connecticut 06830:
Photo album and assorted self-mounting inserts
Paternayan yarn
Domestic canvas

Yarn Center, 60 Greenwich Avenue, Greenwich, Connecticut 06830:
Felt squares
Plastic canvas
Seam binding
DMC embroidery floss
Mohair yarn
Lily cotton crochet yarn

Bibliography

IMPROVING YOUR TECHNIQUE

BUCHER, JO. *Complete Guide to Creative Needlepoint*. Creative Home Library (in association with *Better Homes and Gardens*). Des Moines, Iowa: Meredith Corporation, 1973. (Includes instructions for left-handers.)

BURCHETTE, DOROTHY. *Needlework Blocking and Finishing*. New York: Charles Scribner's Sons, 1974.

HARASZTY, ESZTER, AND COLEN, BRUCE DAVID. *Needlepainting, A Garden of Stitches*. New York: Liveright, 1974.

IREYS, KATHARINE. *The Encyclopedia of Canvas Embroidery Stitch Patterns*. New York: Thomas Y. Crowell Company, 1972.

KARASZ, MARISKA. *Adventures in Stitches*. New York: Funk & Wagnalls, Inc., 1959.

LANTZ, SHERLEE, AND LANE, MAGGIE. *A Pageant of Pattern for Needlepoint Canvas*. New York: Atheneum Publishers, 1973.

DISCOVERING DESIGN

BEVLIN, MAJORIE ELLIOTT. *Design Through Discovery*. New York: Holt, Rinehart and Winston, Inc., 1970.

GOSTELOW, MARY. *A World of Embroidery*. New York: Charles Scribner's Sons, 1975.

HOLSTEIN, JONATHAN. *The Pieced Quilt, An American Design Tradition*. New York: Galahad Books, by arrangement with New York Graphic Society Ltd., 1973.

KRANZ, STEWART, AND FISHER, ROBERT. *The Design Continuum,* New York: Van Nostrand Reinhold Company, 1966.

STIX, HUGH, AND HUGH, MARGUERITE. *The Shell, Five Hundred Million Years of Inspired Design*. New York: Harry N. Abrams, Inc., 1968.

WEAL, MICHELLE. *Color and Texture in Needlepoint*. New York: Harper & Row, Publishers, 1975.

EXPANDING YOUR HORIZONS

ESTEVE, SIRIO. *The Experience*. New York: Random House, Inc., 1974.

MAY, ROLLO. *The Courage to Create*. New York: W. W. Norton & Company, Inc., 1975.

PEARSON, JOHN. *The Sun's Birthday*. Garden City. N.Y.: Doubleday & Company, Inc., 1973.

PINTAURO, JOSEPH, AND KENT, CORITA. *To Believe in Man*. New York: Harper & Row, Publishers, 1970.

RING, BETTY, ed. *Needlework: An Historical Survey*. New York: Universe Books, Inc., 1975.

SWAIN, MARGARET. *The Needlework of Mary Queen of Scots*. New York: Van Nostrand Reinhold Company, Inc., 1973.